The O

by

Sophocles

www.books.com.co

First Printing March 2016
Printed in the United States of America.
10 9 8 7 6 5 4 3 2 1

If this is a work of fiction, it is not meant to depict, portray or represent any particular real persons. All the characters, incidents and dialogues are the products of the author's imagination and are not to be construed as real. Any references or similarities to actual events, entities, real people, living or dead, or to real locales are intended to give the novel a sense of reality. Any similarity in other names, characters, entities, places and incidents is entirely coincidental.

LG Classics
New York, New York
www.books.com.co

ARGUMENT

To Laius, King of Thebes, an oracle foretold that the child born to him by his queen Jocasta would slay his father and wed his mother. So when in time a son was born the infant's feet were riveted together and he was left to die on Mount Cithaeron. But a shepherd found the babe and tended him, and delivered him to another shepherd who took him to his master, the King of Corinth. Polybus being childless adopted the boy, who grew up believing that he was indeed the King's son. Afterwards doubting his parentage he inquired of the Delphic god and heard himself the word declared before to Laius. Wherefore he fled from what he deemed his father's house and in his flight he encountered and unwillingly slew his father Laius. Arriving at Thebes he answered the riddle of the Sphinx and the grateful Thebans made their deliverer king. So he reigned in the room of Laius, and espoused the widowed queen. Children were born to them and Thebes prospered under his rule, but again a grievous plague fell upon the city. Again the oracle was consulted and it bade them purge themselves of blood-guiltiness. Oedipus denounces the crime of which he is unaware, and undertakes to track out the criminal. Step by step it is brought home to him that he is the man. The closing scene reveals Jocasta slain by her own hand and Oedipus blinded by his own act and praying for death or exile.

DRAMATIS PERSONAE

Oedipus.

The Priest of Zeus.

Creon.

Chorus of Theban Elders.

Teiresias.

Jocasta.

Messenger.

Herd of Laius.

Second Messenger.

Scene: Thebes. Before the Palace of Oedipus.

OEDIPUS THE KING

Suppliants of all ages are seated round the altar at the palace doors, at their head a PRIEST OF ZEUS. To them enter OEDI-PUS.

OEDIPUS My children, latest born to Cadmus old, Why sit ye here as suppliants, in your hands Branches of olive filleted with wool? What means this reek of incense everywhere, And everywhere laments and litanies? Children, it were not meet that I should learn From others, and am hither come, myself, I Oedipus, your world-renowned king. Ho! aged sire, whose venerable locks Proclaim thee spokesman of this company, Explain your mood and purport. Is it dread Of ill that moves you or a boon ye crave? My zeal in your behalf ye cannot doubt; Ruthless indeed were I and obdurate If such petitioners as you I spurned.

PRIEST Yea, Oedipus, my sovereign lord and king, Thou seest how both extremes of age besiege Thy palace altars--fledglings hardly winged, and greybeards bowed with years; priests, as am I of Zeus, and these the flower of our youth. Meanwhile, the common folk, with wreathed boughs Crowd our two market-places, or before Both shrines of Pallas congregate, or where Ismenus gives his oracles by fire. For, as thou seest thyself, our ship of State, Sore buffeted, can no more lift her head, Foundered beneath a weltering surge of blood. A blight is on our harvest in the ear, A blight upon the grazing flocks and herds, A blight on wives in travail; and withal Armed with his blazing torch the God of Plague Hath swooped upon our city emptying The house of Cadmus, and the murky realm Of Pluto is full fed with groans and tears. Therefore, O King, here at thy hearth we sit, I and these children; not as deeming thee A new divinity, but the first of men; First in the common accidents of life, And first in visitations of the Gods. Art thou not he who coming to the town of Cadmus freed us from the tax we paid To the fell songstress? Nor hadst thou received Prompting from us or been by others schooled; No, by a god inspired (so all men deem, And testify) didst thou renew our life. And now, O Oedipus, our peerless king, All we thy votaries beseech thee, find Some succor, whether by a voice from heaven Whispered, or haply known by human wit. Tried counselors, methinks, are aptest found [1] To furnish for the future pregnant rede. Upraise, O chief of men, upraise our State! Look to thy laurels! for thy zeal of yore Our country's savior thou art justly hailed: O never may we thus record thy reign:-- "He raised us up only to cast us down." Uplift us, build our city on a rock. Thy

happy star ascendant brought us luck, O let it not decline! If thou
wouldst rule This land, as now thou reignest, better sure To rule
a peopled than a desert realm. Nor battlements nor galleys aught
avail, If men to man and guards to guard them tail.

OEDIPUS Ah! my poor children, known, ah, known too well,
The quest that brings you hither and your need. Ye sicken all, well
wot I, yet my pain, How great soever yours, outtops it all. Your
sorrow touches each man severally, Him and none other, but I
grieve at once Both for the general and myself and you. Therefore
ye rouse no sluggard from day-dreams. Many, my children, are the
tears I've wept, And threaded many a maze of weary thought. Thus
pondering one clue of hope I caught, And tracked it up; I have sent
Menoeceus' son, Creon, my consort's brother, to inquire Of Pythian
Phoebus at his Delphic shrine, How I might save the State by act or
word. And now I reckon up the tale of days Since he set forth, and
marvel how he fares. 'Tis strange, this endless tarrying, passing
strange. But when he comes, then I were base indeed, If I perform
not all the god declares.

PRIEST Thy words are well timed; even as thou speakest That
shouting tells me Creon is at hand.

OEDIPUS O King Apollo! may his joyous looks Be presage of
the joyous news he brings!

PRIEST As I surmise, 'tis welcome; else his head Had scarce
been crowned with berry-laden bays.

OEDIPUS We soon shall know; he's now in earshot range. [En-
ter CREON] My royal cousin, say, Menoeceus' child, What message
hast thou brought us from the god?

CREON Good news, for e'en intolerable ills, Finding right issue, tend to naught but good.

OEDIPUS How runs the oracle? thus far thy words Give me no
ground for confidence or fear.

CREON If thou wouldst hear my message publicly, I'll tell thee
straight, or with thee pass within.

OEDIPUS Speak before all; the burden that I bear Is more for
these my subjects than myself.

CREON Let me report then all the god declared. King Phoebus
bids us straitly extirpate A fell pollution that infests the land, And

no more harbor an inveterate sore.

OEDIPUS What expiation means he? What's amiss?

CREON Banishment, or the shedding blood for blood. This stain of blood makes shipwreck of our state.

OEDIPUS Whom can he mean, the miscreant thus denounced?

CREON Before thou didst assume the helm of State, The sovereign of this land was Laius.

OEDIPUS I heard as much, but never saw the man.

CREON He fell; and now the god's command is plain: Punish his takers-off, whoe'er they be.

OEDIPUS Where are they? Where in the wide world to find The far, faint traces of a bygone crime?

CREON In this land, said the god; "who seeks shall find; Who sits with folded hands or sleeps is blind."

OEDIPUS Was he within his palace, or afield, Or traveling, when Laius met his fate?

CREON Abroad; he started, so he told us, bound For Delphi, but he never thence returned.

OEDIPUS Came there no news, no fellow-traveler To give some clue that might be followed up?

CREON But one escape, who flying for dear life, Could tell of all he saw but one thing sure.

OEDIPUS And what was that? One clue might lead us far, With but a spark of hope to guide our quest.

CREON Robbers, he told us, not one bandit but A troop of knaves, attacked and murdered him.

OEDIPUS Did any bandit dare so bold a stroke, Unless indeed he were suborned from Thebes?

CREON So 'twas surmised, but none was found to avenge His murder mid the trouble that ensued.

OEDIPUS What trouble can have hindered a full quest, When

royalty had fallen thus miserably?

CREON The riddling Sphinx compelled us to let slide The dim past and attend to instant needs.

OEDIPUS Well, I will start afresh and once again Make dark things clear. Right worthy the concern Of Phoebus, worthy thine too, for the dead; I also, as is meet, will lend my aid To avenge this wrong to Thebes and to the god. Not for some far-off kinsman, but myself, Shall I expel this poison in the blood; For whoso slew that king might have a mind To strike me too with his assassin hand. Therefore in righting him I serve myself. Up, children, haste ye, quit these altar stairs, Take hence your suppliant wands, go summon hither The Theban commons. With the god's good help Success is sure; 'tis ruin if we fail. [Exeunt OEDIPUS and CREON]

PRIEST Come, children, let us hence; these gracious words Forestall the very purpose of our suit. And may the god who sent this oracle Save us withal and rid us of this pest. [Exeunt PRIEST and SUPPLIANTS]

CHORUS (Str. 1) Sweet-voiced daughter of Zeus from thy gold-paved Pythian shrine Wafted to Thebes divine, What dost thou bring me? My soul is racked and shivers with fear.   (Healer of Delos, hear!) Hast thou some pain unknown before, Or with the circling years renewest a penance of yore? Offspring of golden Hope, thou voice immortal, O tell me.

(Ant. 1) First on Athene I call; O Zeus-born goddess, defend! Goddess and sister, befriend, Artemis, Lady of Thebes, high-throned in the midst of our mart! Lord of the death-winged dart! Your threefold aid I crave From death and ruin our city to save. If in the days of old when we nigh had perished, ye drave From our land the fiery plague, be near us now and defend us!

(Str. 2) Ah me, what countless woes are mine! All our host is in decline;Weaponless my spirit lies. Earth her gracious fruits denies; Women wail in barren throes; Life on life downstriken goes, Swifter than the wind bird's flight, Swifter than the Fire-God's might, To the westering shores of Night.

(Ant. 2) Wasted thus by death on death All our city perisheth. Corpses spread infection round; None to tend or mourn is found. Wailing on the altar stair Wives and grandams rend the air-- Long-drawn moans and piercing cries Blent with prayers and litanies. Golden child of Zeus, O hear Let thine angel face appear!

(Str. 3) And grant that Ares whose hot breath I feel,
Though without targe or steel He stalks, whose voice is as the battle shout, May turn in sudden rout, To the unharbored Thracian waters sped, Or Amphitrite's bed. For what night leaves undone, Smit by the morrow's sun Perisheth. Father Zeus, whose hand Doth wield the lightning brand, Slay him beneath thy levin bold, we pray, Slay him, O slay!

(Ant. 3) O that thine arrows too, Lycean King, From that taut bow's gold string, Might fly abroad, the champions of our rights; Yea, and the flashing lights Of Artemis, wherewith the huntress sweeps Across the Lycian steeps. Thee too I call with golden-snooded hair, Whose name our land doth bear, Bacchus to whom thy Maenads Evoe shout; Come with thy bright torch, rout, Blithe god whom we adore, The god whom gods abhor.

[Enter OEDIPUS.] OEDIPUS Ye pray; 'tis well, but would ye hear my words And heed them and apply the remedy, Ye might perchance find comfort and relief. Mind you, I speak as one who comes a stranger To this report, no less than to the crime; For how unaided could I track it far Without a clue? Which lacking (for too late Was I enrolled a citizen of Thebes) This proclamation I address to all:-- Thebans, if any knows the man by whom Laius, son of Labdacus, was slain, I summon him to make clean shrift to me. And if he shrinks, let him reflect that thus Confessing he shall 'scape the capital charge; For the worst penalty that shall befall him Is banishment--unscathed he shall depart. But if an alien from a foreign land Be known to any as the murderer, Let him who knows speak out, and he shall have Due recompense from me and thanks to boot. But if ye still keep silence, if through fear For self or friends ye disregard my hest, Hear what I then resolve; I lay my ban On the assassin whosoe'er he be. Let no man in this land, whereof I hold The sovereign rule, harbor or speak to him; Give him no part in prayer or sacrifice Or lustral rites, but hound him from your homes. For this is our defilement, so the god Hath lately shown to me by oracles. Thus as their champion I maintain the cause Both of the god and of the murdered King. And on the murderer this curse I lay (On him and all the partners in his guilt):-- Wretch, may he pine in utter wretchedness! And for myself, if with my privity He gain admittance to my hearth, I pray The curse I laid on others fall on me. See that ye give effect to all my hest, For my sake and the god's and for our land, A desert blasted by the wrath of heaven. For, let alone the god's express command, It were a scandal ye should leave unpurged The murder of a great man and your king, Nor track it home. And now that I am lord, Successor to his throne, his bed, his wife, (And had he not been frustrate in the hope Of issue, common children of one womb Had forced a closer bond twixt him and me, But Fate swooped down upon him), therefore I His blood-avenger will maintain his cause As though he were my sire, and leave no stone Unturned to track the assassin or avenge The son of Labdacus, of Polydore, Of Cadmus, and Agenor first of the race. And for the disobedient thus I pray: May the gods send them neither timely fruits Of earth, nor teeming increase of the womb, But may they waste and pine, as now they waste, Aye and worse stricken; but to all of you, My loyal subjects who approve my acts, May Justice, our ally, and all the gods Be gracious and attend you evermore.

CHORUS The oath thou profferest, sire, I take and swear. I slew him not myself, nor can I name The slayer. For the quest, 'twere well, methinks That Phoebus, who proposed the riddle, himself Should give the answer--who the murderer was.

OEDIPUS Well argued; but no living man can hope To force the gods to speak against their will.

CHORUS May I then say what seems next best to me?

OEDIPUS Aye, if there be a third best, tell it too.

CHORUS My liege, if any man sees eye to eye With our lord Phoebus, 'tis our prophet, lord Teiresias; he of all men best might guide A searcher of this matter to the light.

OEDIPUS Here too my zeal has nothing lagged, for twice At Creon's instance have I sent to fetch him, And long I marvel why he is not here.

CHORUS I mind me too of rumors long ago-- Mere gossip.

OEDIPUS Tell them, I would fain know all.

CHORUS 'Twas said he fell by travelers.

OEDIPUS So I heard, But none has seen the man who saw him fall.

CHORUS Well, if he knows what fear is, he will quail And flee before the terror of thy curse.

OEDIPUS Words scare not him who blenches not at deeds.

CHORUS But here is one to arraign him. Lo, at length They bring the god-inspired seer in whom Above all other men is truth inborn. [Enter TEIRESIAS, led by a boy.]

OEDIPUS Teiresias, seer who comprehendest all, Lore of the wise and hidden mysteries, High things of heaven and low things of the earth, Thou knowest, though thy blinded eyes see naught, What plague infects our city; and we turn To thee, O seer, our one defense and shield. The purport of the answer that the God Returned to us who sought his oracle, The messengers have doubtless told thee--how One course alone could rid us of the pest, To find the murderers of Laius, And slay them or expel them from the land. Therefore begrudging neither augury Nor other divination that is thine, O save thyself, thy country, and thy king, Save all from this defilement of blood shed. On thee we rest. This is man's highest end, To others' service all his powers to lend.

TEIRESIAS Alas, alas, what misery to be wise When wisdom profits nothing! This old lore I had forgotten; else I were not here.

OEDIPUS What ails thee? Why this melancholy mood?

TEIRESIAS Let me go home; prevent me not; 'twere best That thou shouldst bear thy burden and I mine.

OEDIPUS For shame! no true-born Theban patriot Would thus withhold the word of prophecy.

TEIRESIAS Thy words, O king, are wide of the mark, and I For fear lest I too trip like thee...

OEDIPUS Oh speak, Withhold not, I adjure thee, if thou know'st, Thy knowledge. We are all thy suppliants.

TEIRESIAS Aye, for ye all are witless, but my voice Will ne'er reveal my miseries--or thine. [2]

OEDIPUS What then, thou knowest, and yet willst not speak! Wouldst thou betray us and destroy the State?

TEIRESIAS I will not vex myself nor thee. Why ask Thus idly what from me thou shalt not learn?

OEDIPUS Monster! thy silence would incense a flint. Will nothing loose thy tongue? Can nothing melt thee, Or shake thy dogged taciturnity?

TEIRESIAS Thou blam'st my mood and seest not thine own Wherewith thou art mated; no, thou taxest me.

OEDIPUS And who could stay his choler when he heard How insolently thou dost flout the State?

TEIRESIAS Well, it will come what will, though I be mute.

OEDIPUS Since come it must, thy duty is to tell me.

TEIRESIAS I have no more to say; storm as thou willst, And give the rein to all thy pent-up rage.

OEDIPUS Yea, I am wroth, and will not stint my words, But speak my whole mind. Thou methinks thou art he, Who planned the crime, aye, and performed it too, All save the assassination; and if thou Hadst not been blind, I had been sworn to boot That thou alone didst do the bloody deed.

TEIRESIAS Is it so? Then I charge thee to abide By thine own proclamation; from this day Speak not to these or me. Thou art the man, Thou the accursed polluter of this land.

OEDIPUS Vile slanderer, thou blurtest forth these taunts, And think'st forsooth as seer to go scot free.

TEIRESIAS Yea, I am free, strong in the strength of truth.

OEDIPUS Who was thy teacher? not methinks thy art.

TEIRESIAS Thou, goading me against my will to speak.

OEDIPUS What speech? repeat it and resolve my doubt.

TEIRESIAS Didst miss my sense wouldst thou goad me on?

OEDIPUS I but half caught thy meaning; say it again.

TEIRESIAS I say thou art the murderer of the man Whose murderer thou pursuest.

OEDIPUS Thou shalt rue it Twice to repeat so gross a calumny.

TEIRESIAS Must I say more to aggravate thy rage?

OEDIPUS Say all thou wilt; it will be but waste of breath.

TEIRESIAS I say thou livest with thy nearest kin In infamy, unwitting in thy shame.

OEDIPUS Think'st thou for aye unscathed to wag thy tongue?

TEIRESIAS Yea, if the might of truth can aught prevail. OEDIPUS With other men, but not with thee, for thou In ear, wit, eye, in everything art blind.

TEIRESIAS Poor fool to utter gibes at me which all Here present will cast back on thee ere long.

OEDIPUS Offspring of endless Night, thou hast no power O'er me or any man who sees the sun.

TEIRESIAS No, for thy weird is not to fall by me. I leave to Apollo what concerns the god.

OEDIPUS Is this a plot of Creon, or thine own?

TEIRESIAS Not Creon, thou thyself art thine own bane.

OEDIPUS O wealth and empiry and skill by skill Outwitted in the battlefield of life, What spite and envy follow in your train! See, for this crown the State conferred on me. A gift, a thing I sought not, for this crown The trusty Creon, my familiar friend, Hath lain in wait to oust me and suborned This mountebank, this juggling charlatan, This tricksy beggar-priest, for gain alone Keen-eyed, but in his proper art stone-blind. Say, sirrah, hast thou ever proved thyself A prophet? When the riddling Sphinx was here Why hadst thou no deliverance for this folk? And yet the riddle was not to be solved By guess-work but required the prophet's art; Wherein thou wast found lacking; neither birds Nor sign from heaven helped thee, but I came, The simple Oedipus; I stopped her mouth By mother wit, untaught of auguries. This is the man whom thou wouldst undermine, In hope to reign with Creon in my stead. Methinks that thou and thine abettor soon Will rue your plot to drive the scapegoat out. Thank thy grey hairs that thou hast still to learn What chastisement such arrogance deserves.

CHORUS To us it seems that both the seer and thou, O Oedipus, have spoken angry words. This is no time to wrangle but consult How best we may fulfill the oracle.

TEIRESIAS King as thou art, free speech at least is mine To make reply; in this I am thy peer. I own no lord but Loxias; him I serve And ne'er can stand enrolled as Creon's man. Thus then I answer: since thou hast not spared To twit me with my blindness--thou hast eyes, Yet see'st not in what misery thou art fallen, Nor where thou dwellest nor with whom for mate. Dost know thy lineage? Nay, thou know'st it not, And all unwitting art a double foe To thine own kin, the living and the dead; Aye and the dogging curse of mother and sire One day shall drive thee, like a two-edged sword, Beyond our borders, and the eyes that now See clear shall henceforward endless night. Ah whither shall thy bitter cry not reach, What crag in all Cithaeron but shall then Reverberate thy wail, when thou hast found With what a hymeneal thou wast borne Home, but to no fair haven, on the gale! Aye, and a flood of ills thou guessest not Shall set thyself and children in one line. Flout then both Creon and my words, for none Of mortals shall be striken worse than thou.

OEDIPUS Must I endure this fellow's insolence? A murrain on thee! Get thee hence! Begone Avaunt! and never cross my threshold more.

TEIRESIAS I ne'er had come hadst thou not bidden me.

OEDIPUS I know not thou wouldst utter folly, else Long hadst thou waited to be summoned here.

TEIRESIAS Such am I--as it seems to thee a fool, But to the parents who begat thee, wise.

OEDIPUS What sayest thou--"parents"? Who begat me, speak?

TEIRESIAS This day shall be thy birth-day, and thy grave.

OEDIPUS Thou lov'st to speak in riddles and dark words.

TEIRESIAS In reading riddles who so skilled as thou?

OEDIPUS Twit me with that wherein my greatness lies.

TEIRESIAS And yet this very greatness proved thy bane.

OEDIPUS No matter if I saved the commonwealth.

TEIRESIAS 'Tis time I left thee. Come, boy, take me home.

OEDIPUS Aye, take him quickly, for his presence irks And lets me; gone, thou canst not plague me more.

TEIRESIAS I go, but first will tell thee why I came. Thy frown

I dread not, for thou canst not harm me. Hear then: this man whom thou hast sought to arrest With threats and warrants this long while, the wretch Who murdered Laius--that man is here. He passes for an alien in the land But soon shall prove a Theban, native born. And yet his fortune brings him little joy; For blind of seeing, clad in beggar's weeds, For purple robes, and leaning on his staff, To a strange land he soon shall grope his way. And of the children, inmates of his home, He shall be proved the brother and the sire, Of her who bare him son and husband both, Co-partner, and assassin of his sire. Go in and ponder this, and if thou find That I have missed the mark, henceforth declare I have no wit nor skill in prophecy. [Exeunt TEIRESIAS and OEDIPUS]

CHORUS (Str. 1) Who is he by voice immortal named from Pythia's rocky cell, Doer of foul deeds of bloodshed, horrors that no tongue can tell? A foot for flight he needs Fleeter than storm-swift steeds, For on his heels doth follow, Armed with the lightnings of his Sire, Apollo. Like sleuth-hounds too The Fates pursue.

(Ant. 1) Yea, but now flashed forth the summons from Parnassus' snowy peak, "Near and far the undiscovered doer of this murder seek!" Now like a sullen bull he roves Through forest brakes and upland groves, And vainly seeks to fly The doom that ever nigh Flits o'er his head, Still by the avenging Phoebus sped, The voice divine, From Earth's mid shrine. (Str. 2) Sore perplexed am I by the words of the master seer. Are they true, are they false? I know not and bridle my tongue for fear, Fluttered with vague surmise; nor present nor future is clear. Quarrel of ancient date or in days still near know I none Twixt the Labdacidan house and our ruler, Polybus' son. Proof is there none: how then can I challenge our King's good name, How in a blood-feud join for an untracked deed of shame?

(Ant. 2) All wise are Zeus and Apollo, and nothing is hid from their ken; They are gods; and in wits a man may surpass his fellow men; But that a mortal seer knows more than I know--where Hath this been proven? Or how without sign assured, can I blame Him who saved our State when the winged songstress came, Tested and tried in the light of us all, like gold assayed? How can I now assent when a crime is on Oedipus laid?

CREON Friends, countrymen, I learn King Oedipus Hath laid against me a most grievous charge, And come to you protesting. If he deems That I have harmed or injured him in aught By word or deed in this our present trouble, I care not to prolong the span of life, Thus ill-reputed; for the calumny Hits not a single blot, but blasts my name, If by the general voice I am denounced False to the State and false by you my friends.

CHORUS This taunt, it well may be, was blurted out In petulance, not spoken advisedly.

CREON Did any dare pretend that it was I Prompted the seer to utter a forged charge?

CHORUS Such things were said; with what intent I know not.

CREON Were not his wits and vision all astray When upon me he fixed this monstrous charge?

CHORUS I know not; to my sovereign's acts I am blind. But lo, he comes to answer for himself. [Enter OEDIPUS.]

OEDIPUS Sirrah, what mak'st thou here? Dost thou presume To approach my doors, thou brazen-faced rogue, My murderer and the filcher of my crown? Come, answer this, didst thou detect in me Some touch of cowardice or witlessness, That made thee undertake this enterprise? I seemed forsooth too simple to perceive The serpent stealing on me in the dark, Or else too weak to scotch it when I saw. This thou art witless seeking to possess Without a following or friends the crown, A prize that followers and wealth must win.

CREON Attend me. Thou hast spoken, 'tis my turn To make reply. Then having heard me, judge.

OEDIPUS Thou art glib of tongue, but I am slow to learn Of thee; I know too well thy venomous hate.

CREON First I would argue out this very point.

OEDIPUS O argue not that thou art not a rogue.

CREON If thou dost count a virtue stubbornness, Unschooled by reason, thou art much astray.

OEDIPUS If thou dost hold a kinsman may be wronged, And no pains follow, thou art much to seek.

CREON Therein thou judgest rightly, but this wrong That thou allegest--tell me what it is.

OEDIPUS Didst thou or didst thou not advise that I Should call the priest?

CREON   Yes, and I stand to it.

OEDIPUS Tell me how long is it since Laius...

CREON Since Laius...? I follow not thy drift.

OEDIPUS By violent hands was spirited away.

CREON In the dim past, a many years agone.

OEDIPUS Did the same prophet then pursue his craft?

CREON Yes, skilled as now and in no less repute.

OEDIPUS Did he at that time ever glance at me?

CREON Not to my knowledge, not when I was by.

OEDIPUS But was no search and inquisition made?

CREON Surely full quest was made, but nothing learnt.

OEDIPUS Why failed the seer to tell his story then?

CREON I know not, and not knowing hold my tongue.

OEDIPUS This much thou knowest and canst surely tell.

CREON What's mean'st thou? All I know I will declare.

OEDIPUS But for thy prompting never had the seer Ascribed
to me the death of Laius.

CREON If so he thou knowest best; but I Would put thee to the
question in my turn.

OEDIPUS Question and prove me murderer if thou canst.

CREON Then let me ask thee, didst thou wed my sister?

OEDIPUS A fact so plain I cannot well deny.

CREON And as thy consort queen she shares the throne?

OEDIPUS I grant her freely all her heart desires.

CREON And with you twain I share the triple rule?

OEDIPUS Yea, and it is that proves thee a false friend.

CREON Not so, if thou wouldst reason with thyself, As I with
myself. First, I bid thee think, Would any mortal choose a trou-

bled reign Of terrors rather than secure repose, If the same power were given him? As for me, I have no natural craving for the name Of king, preferring to do kingly deeds, And so thinks every sober-minded man. Now all my needs are satisfied through thee, And I have naught to fear; but were I king, My acts would oft run counter to my will. How could a title then have charms for me Above the sweets of boundless influence? I am not so infatuate as to grasp The shadow when I hold the substance fast. Now all men cry me Godspeed! wish me well, And every suitor seeks to gain my ear, If he would hope to win a grace from thee. Why should I leave the better, choose the worse? That were sheer madness, and I am not mad. No such ambition ever tempted me, Nor would I have a share in such intrigue. And if thou doubt me, first to Delphi go, There ascertain if my report was true Of the god's answer; next investigate If with the seer I plotted or conspired, And if it prove so, sentence me to death, Not by thy voice alone, but mine and thine. But O condemn me not, without appeal, On bare suspicion. 'Tis not right to adjudge Bad men at random good, or good men bad. I would as lief a man should cast away The thing he counts most precious, his own life, As spurn a true friend. Thou wilt learn in time The truth, for time alone reveals the just; A villain is detected in a day.

CHORUS To one who walketh warily his words Commend themselves; swift counsels are not sure.

OEDIPUS When with swift strides the stealthy plotter stalks I must be quick too with my counterplot. To wait his onset passively, for him Is sure success, for me assured defeat.

CREON What then's thy will? To banish me the land?

OEDIPUS I would not have thee banished, no, but dead, That men may mark the wages envy reaps.

CREON I see thou wilt not yield, nor credit me.

OEDIPUS [None but a fool would credit such as thou.] [3]

CREON Thou art not wise.

OEDIPUS Wise for myself at least.

CREON Why not for me too?

OEDIPUS Why for such a knave?

CREON Suppose thou lackest sense.

OEDIPUS Yet kings must rule.

CREON Not if they rule ill.

OEDIPUS Oh my Thebans, hear him!

CREON Thy Thebans? am not I a Theban too?

CHORUS Cease, princes; lo there comes, and none too soon, Jocasta from the palace. Who so fit As peacemaker to reconcile your feud? [Enter JOCASTA.]

JOCASTA Misguided princes, why have ye upraised This wordy wrangle? Are ye not ashamed, While the whole land lies striken, thus to voice Your private injuries? Go in, my lord; Go home, my brother, and forebear to make A public scandal of a petty grief.

CREON My royal sister, Oedipus, thy lord, Hath bid me choose (O dread alternative!) An outlaw's exile or a felon's death.

OEDIPUS Yes, lady; I have caught him practicing Against my royal person his vile arts.

CREON May I ne'er speed but die accursed, if I In any way am guilty of this charge.

JOCASTA Believe him, I adjure thee, Oedipus, First for his solemn oath's sake, then for mine, And for thine elders' sake who wait on thee.

CHORUS (Str. 1) Hearken, King, reflect, we pray thee, but not stubborn but relent.

OEDIPUS Say to what should I consent?

CHORUS Respect a man whose probity and troth Are known to all and now confirmed by oath.

OEDIPUS Dost know what grace thou cravest?

CHORUS Yea, I know.

OEDIPUS Declare it then and make thy meaning plain.

CHORUS Brand not a friend whom babbling tongues assail; Let not suspicion 'gainst his oath prevail.

OEDIPUS Bethink you that in seeking this ye seek In very sooth my death or banishment?

CHORUS No, by the leader of the host divine! (Str. 2) Witness, thou Sun, such thought was never mine, Unblest, unfriended may I perish, If ever I such wish did cherish! But O my heart is desolate Musing on our striken State, Doubly fall'n should discord grow Twixt you twain, to crown our woe.

OEDIPUS Well, let him go, no matter what it cost me, Or certain death or shameful banishment, For your sake I relent, not his; and him, Where'er he be, my heart shall still abhor.

CREON Thou art as sullen in thy yielding mood As in thine anger thou wast truculent. Such tempers justly plague themselves the most.

OEDIPUS Leave me in peace and get thee gone.

CREON   I go, By thee misjudged, but justified by these. [Exeunt CREON]

CHORUS (Ant. 1) Lady, lead indoors thy consort; wherefore longer here delay?

JOCASTA Tell me first how rose the fray.

CHORUS Rumors bred unjust suspicious and injustice rankles sore.

JOCASTA Were both at fault?

CHORUS   Both.

JOCASTA What was the tale?

CHORUS Ask me no more. The land is sore distressed; 'Twere better sleeping ills to leave at rest.

OEDIPUS Strange counsel, friend! I know thou mean'st me well, And yet would'st mitigate and blunt my zeal.

CHORUS (Ant. 2) King, I say it once again, Witless were I proved, insane, If I lightly put away Thee my country's prop and stay, Pilot who, in danger sought, To a quiet haven brought Our distracted State; and now Who can guide us right but thou?

JOCASTA Let me too, I adjure thee, know, O king, What cause has stirred this unrelenting wrath.

OEDIPUS I will, for thou art more to me than these. Lady, the cause is Creon and his plots.

JOCASTA But what provoked the quarrel? make this clear.

OEDIPUS He points me out as Laius' murderer.

JOCASTA Of his own knowledge or upon report?

OEDIPUS He is too cunning to commit himself, And makes a mouthpiece of a knavish seer.

JOCASTA Then thou mayest ease thy conscience on that score. Listen and I'll convince thee that no man Hath scot or lot in the prophetic art. Here is the proof in brief. An oracle Once came to Laius (I will not say 'Twas from the Delphic god himself, but from His ministers) declaring he was doomed To perish by the hand of his own son, A child that should be born to him by me. Now Laius--so at least report affirmed-- Was murdered on a day by highwaymen, No natives, at a spot where three roads meet. As for the child, it was but three days old, When Laius, its ankles pierced and pinned Together, gave it to be cast away By others on the trackless mountain side. So then Apollo brought it not to pass The child should be his father's murderer, Or the dread terror find accomplishment, And Laius be slain by his own son. Such was the prophet's horoscope. O king, Regard it not. Whate'er the god deems fit To search, himself unaided will reveal.

OEDIPUS What memories, what wild tumult of the soul Came o'er me, lady, as I heard thee speak!

JOCASTA What mean'st thou? What has shocked and startled thee?

OEDIPUS Methought I heard thee say that Laius Was murdered at the meeting of three roads.

JOCASTA So ran the story that is current still.

OEDIPUS Where did this happen? Dost thou know the place?

JOCASTA Phocis the land is called; the spot is where Branch roads from Delphi and from Daulis meet.

OEDIPUS And how long is it since these things befell?

JOCASTA 'Twas but a brief while were thou wast proclaimed Our country's ruler that the news was brought.

OEDIPUS O Zeus, what hast thou willed to do with me!

JOCASTA What is it, Oedipus, that moves thee so?

OEDIPUS Ask me not yet; tell me the build and height Of Laius? Was he still in manhood's prime?

JOCASTA Tall was he, and his hair was lightly strewn With silver; and not unlike thee in form.

OEDIPUS O woe is me! Mehtinks unwittingly I laid but now a dread curse on myself.

JOCASTA What say'st thou? When I look upon thee, my king, I tremble.

OEDIPUS 'Tis a dread presentiment That in the end the seer will prove not blind. One further question to resolve my doubt.

JOCASTA I quail; but ask, and I will answer all.

OEDIPUS Had he but few attendants or a train Of armed retainers with him, like a prince?

JOCASTA They were but five in all, and one of them A herald; Laius in a mule-car rode.

OEDIPUS Alas! 'tis clear as noonday now. But say, Lady, who carried this report to Thebes?

JOCASTA A serf, the sole survivor who returned.

OEDIPUS Haply he is at hand or in the house?

JOCASTA No, for as soon as he returned and found Thee reigning in the stead of Laius slain, He clasped my hand and supplicated me To send him to the alps and pastures, where He might be farthest from the sight of Thebes. And so I sent him. 'Twas an honest slave And well deserved some better recompense.

OEDIPUS Fetch him at once. I fain would see the man.

JOCASTA He shall be brought; but wherefore summon him?

OEDIPUS Lady, I fear my tongue has overrun Discretion; therefore I would question him.

JOCASTA Well, he shall come, but may not I too claim To share the burden of thy heart, my king?

OEDIPUS And thou shalt not be frustrate of thy wish. Now my imaginings have gone so far. Who has a higher claim that thou to hear My tale of dire adventures? Listen then. My sire was Polybus of Corinth, and My mother Merope, a Dorian; And I was held the foremost citizen, Till a strange thing befell me, strange indeed, Yet scarce deserving all the heat it stirred. A roisterer at some banquet, flown with wine, Shouted "Thou art not true son of thy sire." It irked me, but I stomached for the nonce The insult; on the morrow I sought out My mother and my sire and questioned them. They were indignant at the random slur Cast on my parentage and did their best To comfort me, but still the venomed barb Rankled, for still the scandal spread and grew. So privily without their leave I went To Delphi, and Apollo sent me back Baulked of the knowledge that I came to seek. But other grievous things he prophesied, Woes, lamentations, mourning, portents dire; To wit I should defile my mother's bed And raise up seed too loathsome to behold, And slay the father from whose loins I sprang. Then, lady,--thou shalt hear the very truth-- As I drew near the triple-branching roads, A herald met me and a man who sat In a car drawn by colts--as in thy tale-- The man in front and the old man himself Threatened to thrust me rudely from the path, Then jostled by the charioteer in wrath I struck him, and the old man, seeing this, Watched till I passed and from his car brought down Full on my head the double-pointed goad.   Yet was I quits with him and more; one stroke Of my good staff sufficed to fling him clean Out of the chariot seat and laid him prone. And so I slew them every one. But if Betwixt this stranger there was aught in common With Laius, who more miserable than I, What mortal could you find more god-abhorred? Wretch whom no sojourner, no citizen May harbor or address, whom all are bound To harry from their homes. And this same curse Was laid on me, and laid by none but me. Yea with these hands all gory I pollute The bed of him I slew. Say, am I vile? Am I not utterly unclean, a wretch Doomed to be banished, and in banishment Forgo the sight of all my dearest ones, And never tread again my native earth; Or else to wed my mother and slay my sire, Polybus, who begat me and upreared? If one should say, this is the handiwork Of some inhuman power, who could blame His judgment? But, ye pure and awful gods, Forbid, forbid that I should see that day! May I be blotted out from living men Ere such a plague spot set on me its brand!

CHORUS We too, O king, are troubled; but till thou Hast questioned the survivor, still hope on.

OEDIPUS My hope is faint, but still enough survives To bid me bide the coming of this herd.

JOCASTA Suppose him here, what wouldst thou learn of him?

OEDIPUS I'll tell thee, lady; if his tale agrees With thine, I shall have 'scaped calamity.

JOCASTA And what of special import did I say?

OEDIPUS In thy report of what the herdsman said Laius was slain by robbers; now if he Still speaks of robbers, not a robber, I Slew him not; "one" with "many" cannot square. But if he says one lonely wayfarer, The last link wanting to my guilt is forged.

JOCASTA Well, rest assured, his tale ran thus at first, Nor can he now retract what then he said; Not I alone but all our townsfolk heard it. E'en should he vary somewhat in his story, He cannot make the death of Laius In any wise jump with the oracle. For Loxias said expressly he was doomed To die by my child's hand, but he, poor babe, He shed no blood, but perished first himself. So much for divination. Henceforth I Will look for signs neither to right nor left.

OEDIPUS Thou reasonest well. Still I would have thee send And fetch the bondsman hither. See to it.

JOCASTA That will I straightway. Come, let us within. I would do nothing that my lord mislikes. [Exeunt OEDIPUS and JOCASTA]

CHORUS (Str. 1) My lot be still to lead The life of innocence and fly Irreverence in word or deed, To follow still those laws ordained on high Whose birthplace is the bright ethereal sky   N o mortal birth they own, Olympus their progenitor alone: Ne'er shall they slumber in oblivion cold, The god in them is strong and grows not old.

(Ant. 1) Of insolence is bred The tyrant; insolence full blown, With empty riches surfeited, Scales the precipitous height and grasps the throne. Then topples o'er and lies in ruin prone; No foothold on that dizzy steep. But O may Heaven the true patriot keep Who burns with emulous zeal to serve the State. God is my help and hope, on him I wait.

(Str. 2) But the proud sinner, or in word or deed, That will not

Justice heed, Nor reverence the shrine Of images divine, Perdition seize his vain imaginings, If, urged by greed profane, He grasps at ill-got gain, And lays an impious hand on holiest things. Who when such deeds are done Can hope heaven's bolts to shun? If sin like this to honor can aspire, Why dance I still and lead the sacred choir?

(Ant. 2) No more I'll seek earth's central oracle, Or Abae's hallowed cell, Nor to Olympia bring My votive offering. If before all God's truth be not bade plain. O Zeus, reveal thy might, King, if thou'rt named aright Omnipotent, all-seeing, as of old; For Laius is forgot; His weird, men heed it not; Apollo is forsook and faith grows cold. [Enter JOCASTA.]

JOCASTA My lords, ye look amazed to see your queen With wreaths and gifts of incense in her hands. I had a mind to visit the high shrines, For Oedipus is overwrought, alarmed With terrors manifold. He will not use His past experience, like a man of sense, To judge the present need, but lends an ear To any croaker if he augurs ill. Since then my counsels naught avail, I turn To thee, our present help in time of trouble, Apollo, Lord Lycean, and to thee My prayers and supplications here I bring. Lighten us, lord, and cleanse us from this curse! For now we all are cowed like mariners Who see their helmsman dumbstruck in the storm. [Enter Corinthian MESSENGER.]

MESSENGER My masters, tell me where the palace is Of Oedipus; or better, where's the king.

CHORUS Here is the palace and he bides within; This is his queen the mother of his children.

MESSENGER All happiness attend her and the house, Blessed is her husband and her marriage-bed.

JOCASTA My greetings to thee, stranger; thy fair words Deserve a like response. But tell me why Thou comest--what thy need or what thy news.

MESSENGER Good for thy consort and the royal house.

JOCASTA What may it be? Whose messenger art thou?

MESSENGER The Isthmian commons have resolved to make Thy husband king--so 'twas reported there.

JOCASTA What! is not aged Polybus still king?

MESSENGER No, verily; he's dead and in his grave.

JOCASTA What! is he dead, the sire of Oedipus?

MESSENGER If I speak falsely, may I die myself.

JOCASTA Quick, maiden, bear these tidings to my lord. Ye god-sent oracles, where stand ye now! This is the man whom Oedipus long shunned, In dread to prove his murderer; and now He dies in nature's course, not by his hand. [Enter OEDIPUS.]

OEDIPUS My wife, my queen, Jocasta, why hast thou Summoned me from my palace?

JOCASTA Hear this man, And as thou hearest judge what has become Of all those awe-inspiring oracles.

OEDIPUS Who is this man, and what his news for me?

JOCASTA He comes from Corinth and his message this: Thy father Polybus hath passed away.

OEDIPUS What? let me have it, stranger, from thy mouth.

MESSENGER If I must first make plain beyond a doubt My message, know that Polybus is dead.

OEDIPUS By treachery, or by sickness visited?

MESSENGER One touch will send an old man to his rest.

OEDIPUS So of some malady he died, poor man.

MESSENGER Yes, having measured the full span of years.

OEDIPUS Out on it, lady! why should one regard The Pythian hearth or birds that scream i' the air? Did they not point at me as doomed to slay My father? but he's dead and in his grave And here am I who ne'er unsheathed a sword; Unless the longing for his absent son Killed him and so I slew him in a sense. But, as they stand, the oracles are dead-- Dust, ashes, nothing, dead as Polybus.

JOCASTA Say, did not I foretell this long ago?

OEDIPUS Thou didst: but I was misled by my fear.

JOCASTA Then let I no more weigh upon thy soul.

OEDIPUS Must I not fear my mother's marriage bed.

JOCASTA Why should a mortal man, the sport of chance, With no assured foreknowledge, be afraid? Best live a careless life from hand to mouth. This wedlock with thy mother fear not thou. How oft it chances that in dreams a man Has wed his mother! He who least regards Such brainsick phantasies lives most at ease.

OEDIPUS I should have shared in full thy confidence, Were not my mother living; since she lives Though half convinced I still must live in dread.

JOCASTA And yet thy sire's death lights out darkness much.

OEDIPUS Much, but my fear is touching her who lives.

MESSENGER Who may this woman be whom thus you fear?

OEDIPUS Merope, stranger, wife of Polybus.

MESSENGER And what of her can cause you any fear?

OEDIPUS A heaven-sent oracle of dread import.

MESSENGER A mystery, or may a stranger hear it?

OEDIPUS Aye, 'tis no secret. Loxias once foretold That I should mate with mine own mother, and shed With my own hands the blood of my own sire. Hence Corinth was for many a year to me A home distant; and I trove abroad, But missed the sweetest sight, my parents' face.

MESSENGER Was this the fear that exiled thee from home?

OEDIPUS Yea, and the dread of slaying my own sire.

MESSENGER Why, since I came to give thee pleasure, King, Have I not rid thee of this second fear?

OEDIPUS Well, thou shalt have due guerdon for thy pains.

MESSENGER Well, I confess what chiefly made me come Was hope to profit by thy coming home.

OEDIPUS Nay, I will ne'er go near my parents more.

MESSENGER My son, 'tis plain, thou know'st not what thou doest.

OEDIPUS How so, old man? For heaven's sake tell me all.

MESSENGER If this is why thou dreadest to return.

OEDIPUS Yea, lest the god's word be fulfilled in me.

MESSENGER Lest through thy parents thou shouldst be accursed?

OEDIPUS This and none other is my constant dread.

MESSENGER Dost thou not know thy fears are baseless all?

OEDIPUS How baseless, if I am their very son?

MESSENGER Since Polybus was naught to thee in blood.

OEDIPUS What say'st thou? was not Polybus my sire?

MESSENGER As much thy sire as I am, and no more.

OEDIPUS My sire no more to me than one who is naught?

MESSENGER Since I begat thee not, no more did he.

OEDIPUS What reason had he then to call me son?

MESSENGER Know that he took thee from my hands, a gift.

OEDIPUS Yet, if no child of his, he loved me well.

MESSENGER A childless man till then, he warmed to thee.

OEDIPUS A foundling or a purchased slave, this child?

MESSENGER I found thee in Cithaeron's wooded glens.

OEDIPUS What led thee to explore those upland glades?

MESSENGER My business was to tend the mountain flocks.

OEDIPUS A vagrant shepherd journeying for hire?

MESSENGER True, but thy savior in that hour, my son.

OEDIPUS My savior? from what harm? what ailed me then?

MESSENGER Those ankle joints are evidence enow.

OEDIPUS Ah, why remind me of that ancient sore?

MESSENGER I loosed the pin that riveted thy feet.

OEDIPUS Yes, from my cradle that dread brand I bore.

MESSENGER Whence thou deriv'st the name that still is

thine.

OEDIPUS Who did it? I adjure thee, tell me who Say, was it father, mother?

MESSENGER I know not. The man from whom I had thee may know more.

OEDIPUS What, did another find me, not thyself?

MESSENGER Not I; another shepherd gave thee me.

OEDIPUS Who was he? Would'st thou know again the man?

MESSENGER He passed indeed for one of Laius' house.

OEDIPUS The king who ruled the country long ago?

MESSENGER The same: he was a herdsman of the king.

OEDIPUS And is he living still for me to see him?

MESSENGER His fellow-countrymen should best know that.

OEDIPUS Doth any bystander among you know The herd he speaks of, or by seeing him Afield or in the city? answer straight! The hour hath come to clear this business up.

CHORUS Methinks he means none other than the hind Whom thou anon wert fain to see; but that Our queen Jocasta best of all could tell.

OEDIPUS Madam, dost know the man we sent to fetch? Is the same of whom the stranger speaks?

JOCASTA Who is the man? What matter? Let it be. 'Twere waste of thought to weigh such idle words.

OEDIPUS No, with such guiding clues I cannot fail To bring to light the secret of my birth.

JOCASTA Oh, as thou carest for thy life, give o'er This quest. Enough the anguish I endure.

OEDIPUS Be of good cheer; though I be proved the son Of a bondwoman, aye, through three descents Triply a slave, thy honor is unsmirched.

JOCASTA Yet humor me, I pray thee; do not this.

OEDIPUS I cannot; I must probe this matter home.

JOCASTA 'Tis for thy sake I advise thee for the best.

OEDIPUS I grow impatient of this best advice.

JOCASTA Ah mayst thou ne'er discover who thou art!

OEDIPUS Go, fetch me here the herd, and leave yon woman To glory in her pride of ancestry.

JOCASTA O woe is thee, poor wretch! With that last word I leave thee, henceforth silent evermore. [Exit JOCASTA]

CHORUS Why, Oedipus, why stung with passionate grief Hath the queen thus departed? Much I fear From this dead calm will burst a storm of woes.

OEDIPUS Let the storm burst, my fixed resolve still holds, To learn my lineage, be it ne'er so low. It may be she with all a woman's pride Thinks scorn of my base parentage. But I Who rank myself as Fortune's favorite child, The giver of good gifts, shall not be shamed. She is my mother and the changing moons My brethren, and with them I wax and wane. Thus sprung why should I fear to trace my birth? Nothing can make me other than I am.

CHORUS (Str.) If my soul prophetic err not, if my wisdom aught avail, Thee, Cithaeron, I shall hail, As the nurse and foster-mother of our Oedipus shall greet Ere tomorrow's full moon rises, and exalt thee as is meet. Dance and song shall hymn thy praises, lover of our royal race. Phoebus, may my words find grace!

(Ant.) Child, who bare thee, nymph or goddess? sure thy sure was more than man, Haply the hill-roamer Pan. Of did Loxias beget thee, for he haunts the upland wold; Or Cyllene's lord, or Bacchus, dweller on the hilltops cold? Did some Heliconian Oread give him thee, a new-born joy? Nymphs with whom he love to toy?

OEDIPUS Elders, if I, who never yet before Have met the man, may make a guess, methinks I see the herdsman who we long have sought; His time-worn aspect matches with the years Of yonder aged messenger; besides I seem to recognize the men who bring him As servants of my own. But you, perchance, Having in past days known or seen the herd, May better by sure knowledge my surmise.

CHORUS I recognize him; one of Laius' house; A simple hind,

but true as any man. [Enter HERDSMAN.]

OEDIPUS Corinthian, stranger, I address thee first, Is this the man thou meanest!

MESSENGER This is he.

OEDIPUS And now old man, look up and answer all I ask thee. Wast thou once of Laius' house?

HERDSMAN I was, a thrall, not purchased but home-bred.

OEDIPUS What was thy business? how wast thou employed?

HERDSMAN The best part of my life I tended sheep.

OEDIPUS What were the pastures thou didst most frequent?

HERDSMAN Cithaeron and the neighboring alps.

OEDIPUS Then there Thou must have known yon man, at least by fame?

HERDSMAN Yon man? in what way? what man dost thou mean?

OEDIPUS The man here, having met him in past times...

HERDSMAN Off-hand I cannot call him well to mind.

MESSENGER No wonder, master. But I will revive His blunted memories. Sure he can recall What time together both we drove our flocks, He two, I one, on the Cithaeron range, For three long summers; I his mate from spring Till rose Arcturus; then in winter time I led mine home, he his to Laius' folds. Did these things happen as I say, or no?

HERDSMAN 'Tis long ago, but all thou say'st is true.

MESSENGER Well, thou mast then remember giving me A child to rear as my own foster-son?

HERDSMAN Why dost thou ask this question? What of that?

MESSENGER Friend, he that stands before thee was that child.

HERDSMAN A plague upon thee! Hold thy wanton tongue!

OEDIPUS Softly, old man, rebuke him not; thy words Are more

deserving chastisement than his.

HERDSMAN O best of masters, what is my offense?

OEDIPUS Not answering what he asks about the child.

HERDSMAN He speaks at random, babbles like a fool.

OEDIPUS If thou lack'st grace to speak, I'll loose thy tongue.

HERDSMAN For mercy's sake abuse not an old man.

OEDIPUS Arrest the villain, seize and pinion him!

HERDSMAN Alack, alack! What have I done? what wouldst thou further learn?

OEDIPUS Didst give this man the child of whom he asks?

HERDSMAN I did; and would that I had died that day!

OEDIPUS And die thou shalt unless thou tell the truth.

HERDSMAN But, if I tell it, I am doubly lost.

OEDIPUS The knave methinks will still prevaricate.

HERDSMAN Nay, I confessed I gave it long ago.

OEDIPUS Whence came it? was it thine, or given to thee?

HERDSMAN I had it from another, 'twas not mine.

OEDIPUS From whom of these our townsmen, and what house?

HERDSMAN Forbear for God's sake, master, ask no more.

OEDIPUS If I must question thee again, thou'rt lost.

HERDSMAN Well then--it was a child of Laius' house.

OEDIPUS Slave-born or one of Laius' own race?

HERDSMAN Ah me! I stand upon the perilous edge of speech.

OEDIPUS And I of hearing, but I still must hear.

HERDSMAN Know then the child was by repute his own, But she within, thy consort best could tell.

OEDIPUS What! she, she gave it thee?

HERDSMAN   'Tis so, my king.

OEDIPUS With what intent?

HERDSMAN   To make away with it.

OEDIPUS What, she its mother.

HERDSMAN   Fearing a dread weird.

OEDIPUS What weird?

HERDSMAN   'Twas told that he should slay his sire.

OEDIPUS What didst thou give it then to this old man?

HERDSMAN Through pity, master, for the babe. I thought He'd take it to the country whence he came; But he preserved it for the worst of woes. For if thou art in sooth what this man saith, God pity thee! thou wast to misery born.

OEDIPUS Ah me! ah me! all brought to pass, all true! O light, may I behold thee nevermore! I stand a wretch, in birth, in wedlock cursed, A parricide, incestuously, triply cursed! [Exit OEDIPUS]

CHORUS (Str. 1) Races of mortal man Whose life is but a span, I count ye but the shadow of a shade! For he who most doth know Of bliss, hath but the show; A moment, and the visions pale and fade. Thy fall, O Oedipus, thy piteous fall Warns me none born of women blest to call.

(Ant. 1) For he of marksmen best, O Zeus, outshot the rest, And won the prize supreme of wealth and power. By him the vulture maid Was quelled, her witchery laid; He rose our savior and the land's strong tower. We hailed thee king and from that day adored Of mighty Thebes the universal lord.

(Str. 2) O heavy hand of fate! Who now more desolate, Whose tale more sad than thine, whose lot more dire? O Oedipus, discrowned head, Thy cradle was thy marriage bed; One harborage sufficed for son and sire. How could the soil thy father eared so long Endure to bear in silence such a wrong?

(Ant. 2) All-seeing Time hath caught Guilt, and to justice brought The son and sire commingled in one bed. O child of Laius' ill-starred race Would I had ne'er beheld thy face; I raise for thee a dirge as o'er the dead. Yet, sooth to say, through thee I drew new breath, And now through thee I feel a second death. [Enter SEC-

OND MESSENGER.]

SECOND MESSENGER Most grave and reverend senators of Thebes, What Deeds ye soon must hear, what sights behold How will ye mourn, if, true-born patriots, Ye reverence still the race of Labdacus! Not Ister nor all Phasis' flood, I ween, Could wash away the blood-stains from this house, The ills it shrouds or soon will bring to light, Ills wrought of malice, not unwittingly. The worst to bear are self-inflicted wounds.

CHORUS Grievous enough for all our tears and groans Our past calamities; what canst thou add?

SECOND MESSENGER My tale is quickly told and quickly heard. Our sovereign lady queen Jocasta's dead.

CHORUS Alas, poor queen! how came she by her death?

SECOND MESSENGER By her own hand. And all the horror of it, Not having seen, yet cannot comprehend. Nathless, as far as my poor memory serves, I will relate the unhappy lady's woe. When in her frenzy she had passed inside The vestibule, she hurried straight to win The bridal-chamber, clutching at her hair With both her hands, and, once within the room, She shut the doors behind her with a crash. "Laius," she cried, and called her husband dead Long, long ago; her thought was of that child By him begot, the son by whom the sire Was murdered and the mother left to breed With her own seed, a monstrous progeny. Then she bewailed the marriage bed whereon Poor wretch, she had conceived a double brood, Husband by husband, children by her child. What happened after that I cannot tell, Nor how the end befell, for with a shriek Burst on us Oedipus; all eyes were fixed On Oedipus, as up and down he strode, Nor could we mark her agony to the end. For stalking to and fro "A sword!" he cried, "Where is the wife, no wife, the teeming womb That bore a double harvest, me and mine?" And in his frenzy some supernal power (No mortal, surely, none of us who watched him) Guided his footsteps; with a terrible shriek, As though one beckoned him, he crashed against The folding doors, and from their staples forced The wrenched bolts and hurled himself within. Then we beheld the woman hanging there, A running noose entwined about her neck. But when he saw her, with a maddened roar He loosed the cord; and when her wretched corpse Lay stretched on earth, what followed--O 'twas dread! He tore the golden brooches that upheld Her queenly robes, upraised them high and smote Full on his eye-balls, uttering words like these: "No more shall ye behold such sights of woe, Deeds I have suffered and myself have wrought; Henceforward quenched in darkness shall ye see Those ye should ne'er have seen; now blind to those Whom, when I saw, I vainly yearned to know."Such was the burden of his moan, whereto, Not once but oft, he struck with his hand uplift His eyes, and at each stroke the ensanguined orbs Bedewed his beard, not oozing drop by drop, But one black gory downpour, thick as hail. Such evils, issuing from the double source, Have whelmed them both, confounding man and wife. Till now the storied fortune of this house Was fortunate indeed; but from this day Woe, lamentation, ruin, death, disgrace, All ills that can be named, all, all are theirs.

CHORUS But hath he still no respite from his pain?

SECOND MESSENGER He cries, "Unbar the doors and let all Thebes Behold the slayer of his sire, his mother's--" That shameful word my lips may not repeat. He vows to fly self-banished from the land, Nor stay to bring upon his house the curse Himself had uttered; but he has no strength Nor one to guide him, and his torture's more Than man can suffer, as yourselves will see. For lo, the palace portals are unbarred, And soon ye shall behold a sight so sad That he who must abhorred would pity it. [Enter OEDIPUS blinded.]

CHORUS Woeful sight! more woeful none These sad eyes have looked upon. Whence this madness? None can tell Who did cast on thee his spell, prowling all thy life around, Leaping with a demon bound. Hapless wretch! how can I brook On thy misery to look? Though to gaze on thee I yearn, Much to question, much to learn, Horror-struck away I turn.

OEDIPUS Ah me! ah woe is me! Ah whither am I borne! How like a ghost forlorn My voice flits from me on the air! On, on the demon goads. The end, ah where?

CHORUS An end too dread to tell, too dark to see.

OEDIPUS (Str. 1) Dark, dark! The horror of darkness, like a shroud, Wraps me and bears me on through mist and cloud. Ah me, ah me! What spasms athwart me shoot, What pangs of agonizing memory?

CHORUS No marvel if in such a plight thou feel'st The double weight of past and present woes.

OEDIPUS (Ant. 1) Ah friend, still loyal, constant still and kind, Thou carest for the blind. I know thee near, and though bereft of eyes, Thy voice I recognize.

CHORUS O doer of dread deeds, how couldst thou mar Thy vision thus? What demon goaded thee?

OEDIPUS (Str. 2) Apollo, friend, Apollo, he it was That brought these ills to pass; But the right hand that dealt the blow Was mine, none other. How, How, could I longer see when sight Brought no delight?

CHORUS Alas! 'tis as thou sayest.

OEDIPUS Say, friends, can any look or voice Or touch of love henceforth my heart rejoice? Haste, friends, no fond delay, Take the twice cursed away Far from all ken, The man abhorred of gods, accursed of men.

CHORUS O thy despair well suits thy desperate case. Would I had never looked upon thy face!

OEDIPUS (Ant. 2) My curse on him whoe'er unrived The waif's fell fetters and my life revived! He meant me well, yet had he left me there, He had saved my friends and me a world of care.

CHORUS I too had wished it so.

OEDIPUS Then had I never come to shed My father's blood nor climbed my mother's bed; The monstrous offspring of a womb defiled, Co-mate of him who gendered me, and child. Was ever man before afflicted thus, Like Oedipus.

CHORUS I cannot say that thou hast counseled well, For thou wert better dead than living blind.

OEDIPUS What's done was well done. Thou canst never shake My firm belief. A truce to argument. For, had I sight, I know not with what eyes I could have met my father in the shades, Or my poor mother, since against the twain I sinned, a sin no gallows could atone. Aye, but, ye say, the sight of children joys A parent's eyes. What, born as mine were born? No, such a sight could never bring me joy; Nor this fair city with its battlements, Its temples and the statues of its gods, Sights from which I, now wretchedst of all, Once ranked the foremost Theban in all Thebes, By my own sentence am cut off, condemned By my own proclamation 'gainst the wretch, The miscreant by heaven itself declared Unclean--and of the race of Laius. Thus branded as a felon by myself, How had I dared to look you in the face? Nay, had I known a way to choke the springs Of hearing, I had never shrunk to make A dungeon of this miserable frame, Cut off from sight and hearing; for 'tis bliss to bide in regions sorrow cannot reach. Why didst thou harbor me, Cithaeron, why Didst thou not take and slay me? Then I never Had shown to men the secret of my birth. O Polybus, O Corinth, O my home, Home of my ancestors (so wast thou called) How fair a nursling then I seemed, how foul The canker that lay festering in the bud! Now is the blight revealed of root and fruit. Ye triple high-roads, and thou hidden glen, Coppice, and pass where meet the three-branched ways, Ye drank my blood, the life-blood these hands spilt, My father's; do ye call to mind perchance Those deeds of mine ye witnessed and the work I wrought thereafter when I came to Thebes? O fatal wedlock, thou didst give me birth, And, having borne me, sowed again my seed, Mingling the blood of fathers, brothers, children, Brides, wives and mothers, an incestuous brood, All horrors that are wrought beneath the sun, Horrors so foul to name them were unmeet. O, I adjure you, hide me anywhere Far from this land, or slay me straight, or cast me Down to the depths of ocean out of sight. Come hither, deign to touch an abject wretch; Draw near and fear not; I myself must bear The load of guilt that none but I can share. [Enter CREON.]

CREON Lo, here is Creon, the one man to grant Thy prayer by action or advice, for he Is left the State's sole guardian in thy stead.

OEDIPUS Ah me! what words to accost him can I find? What cause has he to trust me? In the past I have bee proved his rancorous enemy.

CREON Not in derision, Oedipus, I come Nor to upbraid thee with thy past misdeeds. (To BYSTANDERS) But shame upon you! if ye feel no sense Of human decencies, at least revere The Sun whose light beholds and nurtures all. Leave not thus nakedly for all to gaze at A horror neither earth nor rain from heaven Nor light will suffer. Lead him straight within, For it is seemly that a kinsman's woes Be heard by kin and seen by kin alone.

OEDIPUS O listen, since thy presence comes to me A shock of glad surprise--so noble thou, And I so vile--O grant me one small boon. I ask it not on my behalf, but thine.

CREON And what the favor thou wouldst crave of me?

OEDIPUS Forth from thy borders thrust me with all speed; Set me within some vasty desert where No mortal voice shall greet me any more.

CREON This had I done already, but I deemed It first behooved me to consult the god.

OEDIPUS His will was set forth fully--to destroy The parricide, the scoundrel; and I am he.

CREON Yea, so he spake, but in our present plight 'Twere better to consult the god anew.

OEDIPUS Dare ye inquire concerning such a wretch?

CREON Yea, for thyself wouldst credit now his word.

OEDIPUS Aye, and on thee in all humility I lay this charge: let her who lies within Receive such burial as thou shalt ordain; Such rites 'tis thine, as brother, to perform. But for myself, O never let my Thebes, The city of my sires, be doomed to bear The burden of my presence while I live. No, let me be a dweller on the hills, On yonder mount Cithaeron, famed as mine, My tomb predestined for me by my sire And mother, while they lived, that I may die Slain as they sought to slay me, when alive. This much I know full surely, nor disease Shall end my days, nor any common chance; For I had ne'er been snatched from death, unless I was predestined to some awful doom.   So be it. I reck not how Fate deals with me But my unhappy children--for my sons Be not concerned, O Creon, they are men, And for themselves, where'er they be, can fend. But for my daughters twain, poor innocent maids, Who ever sat beside me at the board Sharing my viands, drinking of my cup, For them, I pray thee, care, and, if thou willst, O might I feel their touch and make my moan. Hear me, O prince, my noble-hearted prince! Could I but blindly touch them with my hands I'd think they still were mine, as when I saw. [ANTIGONE and ISMENE are led in.] What say I? can it be my pretty ones Whose sobs I hear? Has Creon pitied me And sent me my two darlings? Can this be?

CREON 'Tis true; 'twas I procured thee this delight, Knowing the joy they were to thee of old.

OEDIPUS God speed thee! and as meed for bringing them May Providence deal with thee kindlier Than it has dealt with me! O children mine, Where are ye? Let me clasp you with these hands, A brother's hands, a father's; hands that made Lack-luster sockets of his once bright eyes; Hands of a man who blindly, recklessly, Became your sire by her from whom he sprang. Though I cannot behold you, I must weep In thinking of the evil days to come, The slights and wrongs that men will put upon you. Where'er ye go to feast or festival, No merrymaking will it prove for you, But oft abashed in tears ye will return. And when ye come to marriageable years, Where's the bold wooers who will jeopardize To take unto himself such disrepute As to my children's children still must cling, For what of infamy is lacking here? "Their father slew his father, sowed the seed Where he himself was gendered, and begat These maidens at the source wherefrom he sprang." Such are the gibes that men will cast at you. Who then will wed you? None, I ween, but ye Must pine, poor maids, in single barrenness. O Prince, Menoeceus' son, to thee, I turn, With the it rests to father them, for we Their natural parents, both of us, are lost. O leave them not to wander poor, unwed, Thy kin, nor let them share my low estate. O pity them so young, and but for thee All destitute. Thy hand upon it, Prince. To you, my children I had much to say, Were ye but ripe to hear. Let this suffice: Pray ye may find some home and live content, And may your lot prove happier than your sire's.

CREON Thou hast had enough of weeping; pass within.

OEDIPUS I must obey, Though 'tis grievous.

CREON   Weep not, everything must have its day.

OEDIPUS Well I go, but on conditions.

CREON   What thy terms for going, say.

OEDIPUS Send me from the land an exile.

CREON   Ask this of the gods, not me.

OEDIPUS But I am the gods' abhorrence.

CREON   Then they soon will grant thy plea.

OEDIPUS Lead me hence, then, I am willing.

CREON   Come, but let thy children go.

OEDIPUS Rob me not of these my children!

CREON   Crave not mastery in all, For the mastery that raised thee was thy bane and wrought thy fall.

CHORUS Look ye, countrymen and Thebans, this is Oedipus the great, He who knew the Sphinx's riddle and was mightiest in our state. Who of all our townsmen gazed not on his fame with envious eyes? Now, in what a sea of troubles sunk and overwhelmed he lies! Therefore wait to see life's ending ere thou count one mortal blest; Wait till free from pain and sorrow he has gained his final rest.

FOOTNOTES

[Footnote 1: Dr. Kennedy and others render "Since to men of experience I see that also comparisons of their counsels are in most lively use."]

[Footnote 2: Literally "not to call them thine," but the Greek may be rendered "In order not to reveal thine."]

[Footnote 3: The Greek text that occurs in this place has been lost.]

OEDIPUS AT COLONUS

ARGUMENT

Oedipus, the blind and banished King of Thebes, has come in his wanderings to Colonus, a deme of Athens, led by his daughter Antigone. He sits to rest on a rock just within a sacred grove of the Furies and is bidden depart by a passing native. But Oedipus, instructed by an oracle that he had reached his final resting-place, refuses to stir, and the stranger consents to go and consult the Elders of Colonus (the Chorus of the Play). Conducted to the spot they pity at first the blind beggar and his daughter, but on learning his name they are horror- striken and order him to quit the land. He appeals to the world-famed hospitality of Athens and hints at the blessings that his coming will confer on the State. They agree to await the decision of King Theseus. From Theseus Oedipus craves protection in life and burial in Attic soil; the benefits that will accrue shall be told later. Theseus departs having promised to aid and befriend him. No sooner has he gone than Creon enters with an armed guard who seize Antigone and carry her off (Ismene, the other sister, they have already captured) and he is about to lay hands on Oedipus, when Theseus, who has heard the tumult, hurries up and, upbraiding Creon for his lawless act, threatens to detain him till he has shown where the captives are and restored them. In the next scene Theseus returns bringing with him the res-cued maidens. He informs Oedipus that a stranger who has taken sanctuary at the altar of Poseidon wishes to see him. It is Poly-neices who has come to crave his father's forgiveness and blessing, knowing by an oracle that victory will fall to the side that Oedi-pus espouses. But Oedipus spurns the hypocrite, and invokes a dire curse on both his unnatural sons. A sudden clap of thunder is heard, and as peal follows peal, Oedipus is aware that his hour is come and bids Antigone summon Theseus. Self-guided he leads the way to the spot where death should overtake him, attended by Theseus and his daughters. Halfway he bids his daughters fare-well, and what followed none but Theseus knew. He was not (so the Messenger reports) for the gods took him.

DRAMATIS PERSONAE

OEDIPUS, banished King of Thebes.

ANTIGONE, his daughter.

ISMENE, his daughter.

THESEUS, King of Athens.

CREON, brother of Jocasta, now reigning at Thebes.

POLYNEICES, elder son of Oedipus.

STRANGER, a native of Colonus.

MESSENGER, an attendant of Theseus.

CHORUS, citizens of Colonus.

Scene: In front of the grove of the Eumenides.

OEDIPUS AT COLONUS

Enter the blind OEDIPUS led by his daughter, ANTIGONE.

OEDIPUS Child of an old blind sire, Antigone, What region, say, whose city have we reached? Who will provide today with scanted dole This wanderer? 'Tis little that he craves, And less obtains--that less enough for me; For I am taught by suffering to endure, And the long years that have grown old with me, And last not least, by true nobility. My daughter, if thou seest a resting place On common ground or by some sacred grove, Stay me and set me down. Let us discover Where we have come, for strangers must inquire Of denizens, and do as they are bid.

ANTIGONE Long-suffering father, Oedipus, the towers That fence the city still are faint and far; But where we stand is surely holy ground; A wilderness of laurel, olive, vine; Within a choir or songster nightingales Are warbling. On this native seat of rock Rest; for an old man thou hast traveled far.

OEDIPUS Guide these dark steps and seat me there secure.

ANTIGONE If time can teach, I need not to be told.

OEDIPUS Say, prithee, if thou knowest, where we are.

ANTIGONE Athens I recognize, but not the spot.

OEDIPUS That much we heard from every wayfarer.

ANTIGONE Shall I go on and ask about the place?

OEDIPUS Yes, daughter, if it be inhabited.

ANTIGONE Sure there are habitations; but no need To leave thee; yonder is a man hard by.

OEDIPUS What, moving hitherward and on his way?

ANTIGONE Say rather, here already. Ask him straight The needful questions, for the man is here. [Enter STRANGER]

OEDIPUS O stranger, as I learn from her whose eyes Must serve both her and me, that thou art here Sent by some happy chance to serve our doubts--

STRANGER First quit that seat, then question me at large: The spot thou treadest on is holy ground.

OEDIPUS What is the site, to what god dedicate?

STRANGER Inviolable, untrod; goddesses, Dread brood of Earth and Darkness, here abide.

OEDIPUS Tell me the awful name I should invoke?

STRANGER The Gracious Ones, All-seeing, so our folk Call them, but elsewhere other names are rife.

OEDIPUS Then may they show their suppliant grace, for I From this your sanctuary will ne'er depart.

STRANGER What word is this?

OEDIPUS The watchword of my fate.

STRANGER Nay, 'tis not mine to bid thee hence without Due warrant and instruction from the State.

OEDIPUS Now in God's name, O stranger, scorn me not As a wayfarer; tell me what I crave.

STRANGER Ask; your request shall not be scorned by me.

OEDIPUS How call you then the place wherein we bide?

STRANGER Whate'er I know thou too shalt know; the place Is all to great Poseidon consecrate. Hard by, the Titan, he who bears the torch, Prometheus, has his worship; but the spot Thou treadest, the Brass-footed Threshold named, Is Athens' bastion, and the neighboring lands Claim as their chief and patron yonder knight Colonus, and in common bear his name. Such, stranger, is the spot, to fame unknown, But dear to us its native worshipers.

OEDIPUS Thou sayest there are dwellers in these parts?

STRANGER Surely; they bear the name of yonder god.

OEDIPUS Ruled by a king or by the general voice?

STRANGER The lord of Athens is our over-lord.

OEDIPUS Who is this monarch, great in word and might?

STRANGER Theseus, the son of Aegeus our late king.

OEDIPUS Might one be sent from you to summon him?

STRANGER Wherefore? To tell him aught or urge his coming?

OEDIPUS Say a slight service may avail him much.

STRANGER How can he profit from a sightless man?

OEDIPUS The blind man's words will be instinct with sight.

STRANGER Heed then; I fain would see thee out of harm; For by the looks, marred though they be by fate, I judge thee noble; tarry where thou art, While I go seek the burghers--those at hand, Not in the city. They will soon decide Whether thou art to rest or go thy way. [Exit STRANGER]

OEDIPUS Tell me, my daughter, has the stranger gone?

ANTIGONE Yes, he has gone; now we are all alone, And thou may'st speak, dear father, without fear.

OEDIPUS Stern-visaged queens, since coming to this land First in your sanctuary I bent the knee, Frown not on me or Phoebus, who, when erst He told me all my miseries to come, Spake of this respite after many years, Some haven in a far-off land, a rest Vouchsafed at last by dread divinities. "There," said he, "shalt thou round thy weary life, A blessing to the land wherein thou dwell'st, But to the land that cast thee forth, a curse." And of my weird he promised signs should come, Earthquake, or thunderclap, or lightning flash. And now I recognize as yours the sign That led my wanderings to this your grove; Else had I never lighted on you first, A wineless man on your seat of native rock. O goddesses, fulfill Apollo's word, Grant me some consummation of my life, If haply I appear not all too vile, A thrall to sorrow worse than any slave. Hear, gentle daughters of primeval Night, Hear, namesake of great Pallas; Athens, first Of cities, pity this dishonored shade, The ghost of him who once was Oedipus.

ANTIGONE Hush! for I see some grey-beards on their way, Their errand to spy out our resting-place.

OEDIPUS I will be mute, and thou shalt guide my steps Into the covert from the public road, Till I have learned their drift. A prudent man Will ever shape his course by what he learns. [Enter CHORUS]

CHORUS (Str. 1) Ha! Where is he? Look around! Every nook and corner scan! He the all-presumptuous man, Whither vanished? search the ground! A wayfarer, I ween, A wayfarer, no countryman of ours, That old man must have been; Never had native dared to tempt the Powers, Or enter their demesne, The Maids in awe of whom each mortal cowers, Whose name no voice betrays nor cry, And as we pass them with averted eye, We move hushed lips in reverent piety. But now some godless man, 'Tis rumored, here abides; The precincts through I scan, Yet wot not where he hides, The wretch profane! I search and search in vain.

OEDIPUS I am that man; I know you near Ears to the blind, they say, are eyes.

CHORUS O dread to see and dread to hear!

OEDIPUS Oh sirs, I am no outlaw under ban.

CHORUS Who can he be--Zeus save us!--this old man?

OEDIPUS No favorite of fate, That ye should envy his estate, O, Sirs, would any happy mortal, say, Grope by the light of other eyes his way, Or face the storm upon so frail a stay?

CHORUS (Ant. 1) Wast thou then sightless from thy birth? Evil, methinks, and long Thy pilgrimage on earth. Yet add not curse to curse and wrong to wrong. I warn thee, trespass not Within this hallowed spot, Lest thou shouldst find the silent grassy glade Where offerings are laid, Bowls of spring water mingled with sweet mead. Thou must not stay, Come, come away, Tired wanderer, dost thou heed? (We are far off, but sure our voice can reach.) If aught thou wouldst beseech, Speak where 'tis right; till then refrain from speech.

OEDIPUS Daughter, what counsel should we now pursue?

ANTIGONE We must obey and do as here they do.

OEDIPUS Thy hand then!

ANTIGONE Here, O father, is my hand,

OEDIPUS O Sirs, if I come forth at your command, Let me not suffer for my confidence.

CHORUS (Str. 2) Against thy will no man shall drive thee hence.

OEDIPUS Shall I go further?

CHORUS Aye.

OEDIPUS What further still?

CHORUS Lead maiden, thou canst guide him where we will.

ANTIGONE Follow with blind steps, father, as I lead.

CHORUS In a strange land strange thou art; To her will incline thy heart; Honor whatso'er the State Honors, all she frowns on hate.

OEDIPUS Guide me child, where we may range Safe within the paths of right; Counsel freely may exchange Nor with fate and fortune fight.

CHORUS (Ant. 2) Halt! Go no further than that rocky floor.

OEDIPUS Stay where I now am?

CHORUS Yes, advance no more.

OEDIPUS May I sit down?

CHORUS Move sideways towards the ledge, And sit thee crouching on the scarped edge.

ANTIGONE This is my office, father, O incline--

OEDIPUS Ah me! ah me!

ANTIGONE Thy steps to my steps, lean thine aged frame on mine.

OEDIPUS Woe on my fate unblest!

CHORUS Wanderer, now thou art at rest, Tell me of thy birth and home, From what far country art thou come, Led on thy weary way, declare!

OEDIPUS Strangers, I have no country. O forbear--

CHORUS What is it, old man, that thou wouldst conceal?

OEDIPUS Forbear, nor urge me further to reveal--

CHORUS Why this reluctance?

OEDIPUS Dread my lineage.

CHORUS Say!

OEDIPUS What must I answer, child, ah welladay!

CHORUS Say of what stock thou comest, what man's son--

OEDIPUS Ah me, my daughter, now we are undone!

ANTIGONE Speak, for thou standest on the slippery verge.

OEDIPUS I will; no plea for silence can I urge.

CHORUS Will neither speak? Come, Sir, why dally thus!

OEDIPUS Know'st one of Laius'--

CHORUS   Ha? Who!

OEDIPUS Seed of Labdacus--

CHORUS   Oh Zeus!

OEDIPUS The hapless Oedipus.

CHORUS   Art he?

OEDIPUS Whate'er I utter, have no fear of me.

CHORUS Begone!

OEDIPUS O wretched me!

CHORUS   Begone!

OEDIPUS O daughter, what will hap anon?

CHORUS Forth from our borders speed ye both!

OEDIPUS How keep you then your troth?

CHORUS Heaven's justice never smites Him who ill with ill requites. But if guile with guile contend, Bane, not blessing, is the end. Arise, begone and take thee hence straightway, Lest on our land a heavier curse thou lay.

ANTIGONE O sirs! ye suffered not my father blind, Albeit gracious and to ruth inclined, Knowing the deeds he wrought, not innocent, But with no ill intent; Yet heed a maiden's moan Who pleads for him alone; My eyes, not reft of sight, Plead with you as a daughter's might You are our providence, O make us not go hence! O with a gracious nod Grant us the nigh despaired-of boon we crave? Hear us, O hear, But all that ye hold dear, Wife, children, homestead, hearth and God! Where will you find one, search ye ne'er so well. Who 'scapes perdition if a god impel!

CHORUS Surely we pity thee and him alike Daughter of Oedipus, for your distress; But as we reverence the decrees of Heaven We cannot say aught other than we said.

OEDIPUS O what avails renown or fair repute? Are they not vanity? For, look you, now Athens is held of States the most devout, Athens alone gives hospitality And shelters the vexed stranger, so men say. Have I found so? I whom ye dislodged First from my seat of rock and now would drive Forth from your land, dreading my name alone; For me you surely dread not, nor my deeds, Deeds of a man more sinned against than sinning, As I might well convince you, were it meet To tell my mother's story and my sire's, The cause of this your fear. Yet am I then A villain born because in self-defense, Striken, I struck the striker back again? E'en had I known, no villainy 'twould prove: But all unwitting whither I went, I went-- To ruin; my destroyers knew it well, Wherefore, I pray you, sirs, in Heaven's name, Even as ye bade me quit my seat, defend me. O pay not a lip service to the gods And wrong them of their dues. Bethink ye well, The eye of Heaven beholds the just of men, And the unjust, nor ever in this world Has one sole godless sinner found escape. Stand then on Heaven's side and never blot Athens' fair scutcheon by abetting wrong. I came to you a suppliant, and you pledged Your honor; O preserve me to the end, O let not this marred visage do me wrong! A holy and god-fearing man is here Whose coming purports comfort for your folk. And when your chief arrives, whoe'er he be, Then shall ye have my story and know all. Meanwhile I pray you do me no despite.

CHORUS The plea thou urgest, needs must give us pause, Set forth in weighty argument, but we Must leave the issue with the ruling powers.

OEDIPUS Where is he, strangers, he who sways the realm?

CHORUS In his ancestral seat; a messenger, The same who sent us here, is gone for him.

OEDIPUS And think you he will have such care or thought For the blind stranger as to come himself?

CHORUS Aye, that he will, when once he learns thy name.

OEDIPUS But who will bear him word!

CHORUS The way is long, And many travelers pass to speed the news. Be sure he'll hear and hasten, never fear; So wide and far thy name is noised abroad, That, were he ne'er so spent and loth to move, He would bestir him when he hears of thee.

OEDIPUS Well, may he come with blessing to his State And me! Who serves his neighbor serves himself. [5]

ANTIGONE Zeus! What is this? What can I say or think?

OEDIPUS What now, Antigone?

ANTIGONE I see a woman Riding upon a colt of Aetna's breed; She wears for headgear a Thessalian hat To shade her from the sun. Who can it be? She or a stranger? Do I wake or dream? 'This she; 'tis not--I cannot tell, alack; It is no other! Now her bright'ning glance Greets me with recognition, yes, 'tis she, Herself, Ismene!

OEDIPUS Ha! what say ye, child?

ANTIGONE That I behold thy daughter and my sister, And thou wilt know her straightway by her voice. [Enter ISMENE]

ISMENE Father and sister, names to me most sweet, How hardly have I found you, hardly now When found at last can see you through my tears!

OEDIPUS Art come, my child?

ISMENE   O father, sad thy plight!

OEDIPUS Child, thou art here?

ISMENE   Yes, 'twas a weary way.

OEDIPUS Touch me, my child.

ISMENE   I give a hand to both.

OEDIPUS O children--sisters!

ISMENE   O disastrous plight!

OEDIPUS Her plight and mine?

ISMENE   Aye, and my own no less.

OEDIPUS What brought thee, daughter?

ISMENE   Father, care for thee.

OEDIPUS A daughter's yearning?

ISMENE   Yes, and I had news I would myself deliver, so I came With the one thrall who yet is true to me.

OEDIPUS Thy valiant brothers, where are they at need?

ISMENE They are--enough, 'tis now their darkest hour.

OEDIPUS Out on the twain! The thoughts and actions all Are framed and modeled on Egyptian ways. For there the men sit at the loom indoors While the wives slave abroad for daily bread. So you, my children--those whom I behooved To bear the burden, stay at home like girls, While in their stead my daughters moil and drudge, Lightening their father's misery. The one Since first she grew from girlish feebleness To womanhood has been the old man's guide And shared my weary wandering, roaming oft Hungry and footsore through wild forest ways, In drenching rains and under scorching suns, Careless herself of home and ease, if so Her sire might have her tender ministry. And thou, my child, whilom thou wentest forth, Eluding the Cadmeians' vigilance, To bring thy father all the oracles Concerning Oedipus, and didst make thyself My faithful lieger, when they banished me. And now what mission summons thee from home, What news, Ismene, hast thou for thy father? This much I know, thou com'st not empty-handed, Without a warning of some new alarm.

ISMENE The toil and trouble, father, that I bore To find thy lodging-place and how thou faredst, I spare thee; surely 'twere a double pain To suffer, first in act and then in telling; 'Tis the misfortune of thine ill-starred sons I come to tell thee. At the first they willed To leave the throne to Creon, minded well Thus to remove the inveterate curse of old, A canker that infected all thy race. But now some god and an infatuate soul Have stirred betwixt them a mad rivalry To grasp at sovereignty and kingly power. Today the hot-branded youth, the younger born, Is keeping Polyneices from the throne, His elder, and has thrust him from the land. The banished brother (so all Thebes reports) Fled to the vale of Argos, and by help Of new alliance there and friends in arms, Swears he will stablish Argos straight as lord Of the Cadmeian land, or, if he fail, Exalt the victor to the stars of heaven. This is no empty tale, but deadly truth, My father; and how long thy agony, Ere the gods pity thee, I cannot tell.

OEDIPUS Hast thou indeed then entertained a hope The gods at last will turn and rescue me?

ISMENE Yea, so I read these latest oracles.

OEDIPUS What oracles? What hath been uttered, child?

ISMENE Thy country (so it runs) shall yearn in time To have thee for their weal alive or dead.

OEDIPUS And who could gain by such a one as I?

ISMENE On thee, 'tis said, their sovereignty depends.

OEDIPUS So, when I cease to be, my worth begins.

ISMENE The gods, who once abased, uplift thee now.

OEDIPUS Poor help to raise an old man fallen in youth.

ISMENE Howe'er that be, 'tis for this cause alone That Creon comes to thee--and comes anon.

OEDIPUS With what intent, my daughter? Tell me plainly.

ISMENE To plant thee near the Theban land, and so Keep thee within their grasp, yet now allow Thy foot to pass beyond their boundaries.

OEDIPUS What gain they, if I lay outside?

OEDIPUS Thy tomb, If disappointed, brings on them a curse.

OEDIPUS It needs no god to tell what's plain to sense.

ISMENE Therefore they fain would have thee close at hand, Not where thou wouldst be master of thyself.

OEDIPUS Mean they to shroud my bones in Theban dust?

ISMENE Nay, father, guilt of kinsman's blood forbids.

OEDIPUS Then never shall they be my masters, never!

ISMENE Thebes, thou shalt rue this bitterly some day!

OEDIPUS When what conjunction comes to pass, my child?

ISMENE Thy angry wraith, when at thy tomb they stand. [6]

OEDIPUS And who hath told thee what thou tell'st me, child?

ISMENE Envoys who visited the Delphic hearth.

OEDIPUS Hath Phoebus spoken thus concerning me?

ISMENE So say the envoys who returned to Thebes.

OEDIPUS And can a son of mine have heard of this?

ISMENE Yea, both alike, and know its import well.

OEDIPUS They knew it, yet the ignoble greed of rule Outweighed all longing for their sire's return.

ISMENE Grievous thy words, yet I must own them true.

OEDIPUS Then may the gods ne'er quench their fatal feud, And mine be the arbitrament of the fight, For which they now are arming, spear to spear; That neither he who holds the scepter now May keep this throne, nor he who fled the realm Return again. They never raised a hand, When I their sire was thrust from hearth and home, When I was banned and banished, what recked they? Say you 'twas done at my desire, a grace Which the state, yielding to my wish, allowed? Not so; for, mark you, on that very day When in the tempest of my soul I craved Death, even death by stoning, none appeared To further that wild longing, but anon, When time had numbed my anguish and I felt My wrath had all outrun those errors past, Then, then it was the city went about By force to oust me, respited for years; And then my sons, who should as sons have helped, Did nothing: and, one little word from them Was all I needed, and they spoke no word, But let me wander on for evermore, A banished man, a beggar. These two maids Their sisters, girls, gave all their sex could give, Food and safe harborage and filial care; While their two brethren sacrificed their sire For lust of power and sceptred sovereignty. No! me they ne'er shall win for an ally, Nor will this Theban kingship bring them gain; That know I from this maiden's oracles, And those old prophecies concerning me, Which Phoebus now at length has brought to pass. Come Creon then, come all the mightiest In Thebes to seek me; for if ye my friends, Championed by those dread Powers indigenous, Espouse my cause; then for the State ye gain A great deliverer, for my foemen bane.

CHORUS Our pity, Oedipus, thou needs must move, Thou and these maidens; and the stronger plea Thou urgest, as the savior of our land, Disposes me to counsel for thy weal.

OEDIPUS Aid me, kind sirs; I will do all you bid.

CHORUS First make atonement to the deities, Whose grove by trespass thou didst first profane.

OEDIPUS After what manner, stranger? Teach me, pray.

CHORUS Make a libation first of water fetched With undefiled hands from living spring.

OEDIPUS And after I have gotten this pure draught?

CHORUS Bowls thou wilt find, the carver's handiwork; Crown thou the rims and both the handles crown--

OEDIPUS With olive shoots or blocks of wool, or how?

CHORUS With wool from fleece of yearling freshly shorn.

OEDIPUS What next? how must I end the ritual?

CHORUS Pour thy libation, turning to the dawn.

OEDIPUS Pouring it from the urns whereof ye spake?

CHORUS Yea, in three streams; and be the last bowl drained To the last drop.

OEDIPUS And wherewith shall I fill it, Ere in its place I set it? This too tell.

CHORUS With water and with honey; add no wine.

OEDIPUS And when the embowered earth hath drunk thereof?

CHORUS Then lay upon it thrice nine olive sprays With both thy hands, and offer up this prayer.

OEDIPUS I fain would hear it; that imports the most.

CHORUS That, as we call them Gracious, they would deign To grant the suppliant their saving grace. So pray thyself or whoso pray for thee, In whispered accents, not with lifted voice; Then go and look back. Do as I bid, And I shall then be bold to stand thy friend; Else, stranger, I should have my fears for thee.

OEDIPUS Hear ye, my daughters, what these strangers say?

ANTIGONE We listened, and attend thy bidding, father.

OEDIPUS I cannot go, disabled as I am Doubly, by lack of

strength and lack of sight; But one of you may do it in my stead; For one, I trow, may pay the sacrifice Of thousands, if his heart be leal and true. So to your work with speed, but leave me not Untended; for this frame is all too week To move without the help of guiding hand.

ISMENE Then I will go perform these rites, but where To find the spot, this have I yet to learn.

CHORUS Beyond this grove; if thou hast need of aught, The guardian of the close will lend his aid.

ISMENE I go, and thou, Antigone, meanwhile Must guard our father. In a parent's cause Toil, if there be toil, is of no account. [Exit ISMENE]

CHORUS (Str. 1) Ill it is, stranger, to awake Pain that long since has ceased to ache, And yet I fain would hear--

OEDIPUS What thing?

CHORUS Thy tale of cruel suffering For which no cure was found, The fate that held thee bound.

OEDIPUS O bid me not (as guest I claim This grace) expose my shame.

CHORUS The tale is bruited far and near, And echoes still from ear to ear. The truth, I fain would hear.

OEDIPUS Ah me!

CHORUS I prithee yield.

OEDIPUS Ah me!

CHORUS Grant my request, I granted all to thee.

OEDIPUS (Ant. 1) Know then I suffered ills most vile, but none (So help me Heaven!) from acts in malice done.

CHORUS Say how.

OEDIPUS The State around An all unwitting bridegroom bound An impious marriage chain; That was my bane.

CHORUS Didst thou in sooth then share A bed incestuous with her that bare--

OEDIPUS It stabs me like a sword, That two-edged word, O stranger, but these maids--my own--

CHORUS Say on.

OEDIPUS Two daughters, curses twain.

CHORUS Oh God!

OEDIPUS Sprang from the wife and mother's travail-pain.

CHORUS (Str. 2) What, then thy offspring are at once--

OEDIPUS Too true. Their father's very sister's too.

CHORUS Oh horror!

OEDIPUS Horrors from the boundless deep Back on my soul in refluent surges sweep.

CHORUS Thou hast endured--

OEDIPUS Intolerable woe.

CHORUS And sinned--

OEDIPUS I sinned not.

CHORUS   How so?

OEDIPUS I served the State; would I had never won That graceless grace by which I was undone.

CHORUS (Ant. 2) And next, unhappy man, thou hast shed blood?

OEDIPUS Must ye hear more?

CHORUS   A father's?

OEDIPUS Flood on flood Whelms me; that word's a second mortal blow.

CHORUS Murderer!

OEDIPUS Yes, a murderer, but know--

CHORUS What canst thou plead?

OEDIPUS A plea of justice.

CHORUS How?

OEDIPUS I slew who else would me have slain; I slew without intent, A wretch, but innocent In the law's eye, I stand, without a stain.

CHORUS Behold our sovereign, Theseus, Aegeus' son, Comes at thy summons to perform his part. [Enter THESEUS]

THESEUS Oft had I heard of thee in times gone by-- The bloody mutilation of thine eyes-- And therefore know thee, son of Laius. All that I lately gathered on the way Made my conjecture doubly sure; and now Thy garb and that marred visage prove to me That thou art he. So pitying thine estate, Most ill-starred Oedipus, I fain would know What is the suit ye urge on me and Athens, Thou and the helpless maiden at thy side. Declare it; dire indeed must be the tale Whereat I should recoil. I too was reared, Like thee, in exile, and in foreign lands Wrestled with many perils, no man more. Wherefore no alien in adversity Shall seek in vain my succor, nor shalt thou; I know myself a mortal, and my share In what the morrow brings no more than thine.

OEDIPUS Theseus, thy words so apt, so generous So comfortable, need no long reply Both who I am and of what lineage sprung, And from what land I came, thou hast declared. So without prologue I may utter now My brief petition, and the tale is told.

THESEUS Say on, and tell me what I fain would learn.

OEDIPUS I come to offer thee this woe-worn frame, A gift not fair to look on; yet its worth More precious far than any outward show.

THESEUS What profit dost thou proffer to have brought?

OEDIPUS Hereafter thou shalt learn, not yet, methinks.

THESEUS When may we hope to reap the benefit?

OEDIPUS When I am dead and thou hast buried me.

THESEUS Thou cravest life's last service; all before-- Is it forgotten or of no account?

OEDIPUS Yea, the last boon is warrant for the rest.

THESEUS The grace thou cravest then is small indeed.

OEDIPUS Nay, weigh it well; the issue is not slight.

THESEUS Thou meanest that betwixt thy sons and me?

OEDIPUS Prince, they would fain convey me back to Thebes.

THESEUS If there be no compulsion, then methinks To rest in banishment befits not thee.

OEDIPUS Nay, when I wished it they would not consent.

THESEUS For shame! such temper misbecomes the faller.

OEDIPUS Chide if thou wilt, but first attend my plea.

THESEUS Say on, I wait full knowledge ere I judge.

OEDIPUS O Theseus, I have suffered wrongs on wrongs.

THESEUS Wouldst tell the old misfortune of thy race?

OEDIPUS No, that has grown a byword throughout Greece.

THESEUS What then can be this more than mortal grief?

OEDIPUS My case stands thus; by my own flesh and blood I was expelled my country, and can ne'er Thither return again, a parricide.

THESEUS Why fetch thee home if thou must needs obey.

THESEUS What are they threatened by the oracle?

OEDIPUS Destruction that awaits them in this land.

THESEUS What can beget ill blood 'twixt them and me?

OEDIPUS Dear son of Aegeus, to the gods alone Is given immunity from eld and death; But nothing else escapes all-ruinous time. Earth's might decays, the might of men decays, Honor grows cold, dishonor flourishes, There is no constancy 'twixt friend and friend, Or city and city; be it soon or late, Sweet turns to bitter, hate once more to love. If now 'tis sunshine betwixt Thebes and thee And not a cloud, Time in his endless course Gives birth to endless days and nights, wherein The merest nothing shall suffice to cut With serried spears your bonds of amity. Then shall my slumbering and buried corpse In its cold grave drink their warm life-blood up, If Zeus be Zeus and Phoebus still speak true. No more: 'tis ill to tear aside the veil Of mysteries; let me cease as I began: Enough if thou wilt keep thy plighted troth, Then shall thou ne'er complain that Oedipus Proved an unprofitable and thankless guest, Except the gods themselves shall play me false.

CHORUS The man, my lord, has from the very first Declared his power to offer to our land These and like benefits.

THESEUS Who could reject The proffered amity of such a friend? First, he can claim the hospitality To which by mutual contract we stand pledged: Next, coming here, a suppliant to the gods, He pays full tribute to the State and me; His favors therefore never will I spurn, But grant him the full rights of citizen; And, if it suits the stranger here to bide, I place him in your charge, or if he please Rather to come with me--choose, Oedipus, Which of the two thou wilt. Thy choice is mine.

OEDIPUS Zeus, may the blessing fall on men like these!

THESEUS What dost thou then decide--to come with me?

OEDIPUS Yea, were it lawful--but 'tis rather here--

THESEUS What wouldst thou here? I shall not thwart thy wish.

OEDIPUS Here shall I vanquish those who cast me forth.

THESEUS Then were thy presence here a boon indeed.

OEDIPUS Such shall it prove, if thou fulfill'st thy pledge.

THESEUS Fear not for me; I shall not play thee false.

OEDIPUS No need to back thy promise with an oath.

THESEUS An oath would be no surer than my word.

OEDIPUS How wilt thou act then?

THESEUS What is it thou fear'st?

OEDIPUS My foes will come--

THESEUS Our friends will look to that.

OEDIPUS But if thou leave me?

THESEUS Teach me not my duty.

OEDIPUS 'Tis fear constrains me.

THESEUS My soul knows no fear!

OEDIPUS Thou knowest not what threats--

THESEUS I know that none Shall hale thee hence in my despite. Such threats Vented in anger oft, are blusterers, An idle breath, forgot when sense returns. And for thy foemen, though their words were brave, Boasting to bring thee back, they are like to find The seas between us wide and hard to sail. Such my firm purpose, but in any case Take heart, since Phoebus sent thee here. My name, Though I be distant, warrants thee from harm.

CHORUS (Str. 1) Thou hast come to a steed-famed land for rest, O stranger worn with toil, To a land of all lands the goodliest Colonus' glistening soil. 'Tis the haunt of the clear-voiced nightingale, Who hid in her bower, among The wine-dark ivy that wreathes the vale, Trilleth her ceaseless song; And she loves, where the clustering berries nod O'er a sunless, windless glade, The spot by no mortal footstep trod, The pleasance kept for the Bacchic god, Where he holds each night his revels wild With the nymphs who fostered the lusty child.

(Ant. 1)   And fed each morn by the pearly dew   The starred narcissi shine, And a wreath with the crocus' golden hue For the Mother and Daughter twine. And never the sleepless fountains cease That feed Cephisus' stream, But they swell earth's bosom with quick increase, And their wave hath a crystal gleam. And   the Muses' quire will never disdain To visit this heaven-favored plain, Nor the Cyprian queen of the golden rein.

(Str. 2)   And here there grows, unpruned, untamed, Terror to foemen's spear, A tree in Asian soil unnamed, By Pelops' Dorian isle unclaimed, Self-nurtured year by year; 'Tis the grey-leaved olive that feeds our boys; Nor youth nor withering age destroys The plant that the Olive Planter tends And the Grey-eyed Goddess herself defends.

(Ant. 2)   Yet another gift, of all gifts the most Prized by our fatherland, we boast-- The might of the horse, the might of the sea; Our fame, Poseidon, we owe to thee, Son of Kronos, our king divine, Who in these highways first didst fit For the mouth of horses the iron bit; Thou too hast taught us to fashion meet For the arm of the rower the oar-blade fleet, Swift as the Nereids' hundred feet   A s they dance along the brine.

ANTIGONE Oh land extolled above all lands, 'tis now For thee to make these glorious titles good.

OEDIPUS Why this appeal, my daughter?

ANTIGONE Father, lo! Creon approaches with his company.

OEDIPUS Fear not, it shall be so; if we are old, This country's vigor has no touch of age. [Enter CREON with attendants]

CREON Burghers, my noble friends, ye take alarm At my approach (I read it in your eyes), Fear nothing and refrain from angry words. I come with no ill purpose; I am old, And know the city whither I am come, Without a peer amongst the powers of Greece. It was by reason of my years that I Was chosen to persuade your guest and bring Him back to Thebes; not the delegate Of one man, but commissioned by the State, Since of all Thebans I have most bewailed, Being his kinsman, his most grievous woes. O listen to me, luckless Oedipus, Come home! The whole Cadmeian people claim With right to have thee back, I most of all, For most of all (else were I vile indeed) I mourn for thy misfortunes, seeing thee An aged outcast, wandering on and on, A beggar with one handmaid for thy stay. Ah! who had e'er imagined she could fall To such a depth of misery as this, To tend in penury thy stricken frame, A virgin ripe for wedlock, but unwed, A prey for any wanton ravisher? Seems it not cruel this reproach I cast On thee and on myself and all the race? Aye, but an open shame cannot be hid. Hide it, O hide it, Oedipus, thou canst. O, by our fathers' gods, consent I pray; Come back to Thebes, come to thy father's home, Bid Athens, as is meet, a fond farewell; Thebes thy old foster-mother claims thee first.

OEDIPUS O front of brass, thy subtle tongue would twist To thy advantage every plea of right Why try thy arts on me, why spread again Toils where 'twould gall me sorest to be snared? In old days when by self-wrought woes distraught, I yearned for exile as a glad release, Thy will refused the favor then I craved. But when my frenzied grief had spent its force, And I was fain to taste the sweets of home, Then thou wouldst thrust me from my country, then These ties of kindred were by thee ignored; And now again when thou behold'st this State And all its kindly people welcome me, Thou seek'st to part us, wrapping in soft words Hard thoughts. And yet what pleasure canst thou find In forcing friendship on unwilling foes? Suppose a man refused to grant some boon When you importuned him, and afterwards When you had got your heart's desire, consented, Granting a grace from which all grace had fled,

Would not such favor seem an empty boon? Yet such the boon thou profferest now to me, Fair in appearance, but when tested false. Yea, I will proved thee false, that these may hear; Thou art come to take me, not to take me home, But plant me on thy borders, that thy State May so escape annoyance from this land. That thou shalt never gain, but this instead-- My ghost to haunt thy country without end; And for my sons, this heritage--no more-- Just room to die in. Have not I more skill Than thou to draw the horoscope of Thebes? Are not my teachers surer guides than thine-- Great Phoebus and the sire of Phoebus, Zeus? Thou art a messenger suborned, thy tongue Is sharper than a sword's edge, yet thy speech Will bring thee more defeats than victories. Howbeit, I know I waste my words--begone, And leave me here; whate'er may be my lot, He lives not ill who lives withal content.

CREON Which loses in this parley, I o'erthrown By thee, or thou who overthrow'st thyself?

OEDIPUS I shall be well contented if thy suit Fails with these strangers, as it has with me.

CREON Unhappy man, will years ne'er make thee wise? Must thou live on to cast a slur on age?

OEDIPUS Thou hast a glib tongue, but no honest man, Methinks, can argue well on any side.

CREON 'Tis one thing to speak much, another well.

OEDIPUS Thy words, forsooth, are few and all well aimed!

CREON Not for a man indeed with wits like thine.

OEDIPUS Depart! I bid thee in these burghers' name, And prowl no longer round me to blockade My destined harbor.

CREON   I protest to these, Not thee, and for thine answer to thy kin, If e'er I take thee--

OEDIPUS Who against their will Could take me?

CREON   Though untaken thou shalt smart.

OEDIPUS What power hast thou to execute this threat?

CREON One of thy daughters is already seized, The other I will carry off anon.

OEDIPUS Woe, woe!

CREON   This is but prelude to thy woes.

OEDIPUS Hast thou my child?

CREON   And soon shall have the other.

OEDIPUS Ho, friends! ye will not surely play me false? Chase this ungodly villain from your land.

CHORUS Hence, stranger, hence avaunt! Thou doest wrong In this, and wrong in all that thou hast done.

CREON (to his guards) 'Tis time by force to carry off the girl, If she refuse of her free will to go.

ANTIGONE Ah, woe is me! where shall I fly, where find Succor from gods or men?

CHORUS   What would'st thou, stranger?

CREON I meddle not with him, but her who is mine.

OEDIPUS O princes of the land!

CHORUS   Sir, thou dost wrong.

CREON Nay, right.

CHORUS   How right?

CREON   I take but what is mine.

OEDIPUS Help, Athens!

CHORUS What means this, sirrah? quick unhand her, or We'll fight it out.

CREON   Back!

CHORUS   Not till thou forbear.

CREON 'Tis war with Thebes if I am touched or harmed.

OEDIPUS Did I not warn thee?

CHORUS   Quick, unhand the maid!

CREON Command your minions; I am not your slave.

CHORUS Desist, I bid thee.

CREON (to the guard) And O bid thee march!

CHORUS   To the rescue, one and all! Rally, neighbors to my call! See, the foe is at the gate! Rally to defend the State.

ANTIGONE Ah, woe is me, they drag me hence, O friends.

OEDIPUS Where art thou, daughter?

ANTIGONE Haled along by force.

OEDIPUS Thy hands, my child!

ANTIGONE They will not let me, father.

CREON Away with her!

OEDIPUS Ah, woe is me, ah woe!

CREON So those two crutches shall no longer serve thee For further roaming. Since it pleaseth thee To triumph o'er thy country and thy friends Who mandate, though a prince, I here discharge, Enjoy thy triumph; soon or late thou'lt find Thou art an enemy to thyself, both now And in time past, when in despite of friends Thou gav'st the rein to passion, still thy bane.

CHORUS Hold there, sir stranger!

CREON   Hands off, have a care.

CHORUS Restore the maidens, else thou goest not.

CREON Then Thebes will take a dearer surety soon; I will lay hands on more than these two maids.

CHORUS What canst thou further?

CREON   Carry off this man.

CHORUS Brave words!

CREON   And deeds forthwith shall make them good.

CHORUS Unless perchance our sovereign intervene.

OEDIPUS O shameless voice! Would'st lay an hand on me?

CREON Silence, I bid thee!

OEDIPUS Goddesses, allow Thy suppliant to utter yet one curse! Wretch, now my eyes are gone thou hast torn away The helpless maiden who was eyes to me; For these to thee and all thy cursed race May the great Sun, whose eye is everywhere, Grant length of days and old age like to mine.

CREON Listen, O men of Athens, mark ye this?

OEDIPUS They mark us both and understand that I Wronged by the deeds defend myself with words.

CREON Nothing shall curb my will; though I be old And single-handed, I will have this man.

OEDIPUS O woe is me!

CHORUS Thou art a bold man, stranger, if thou think'st To execute thy purpose.

CREON   So I do.

CHORUS Then shall I deem this State no more a State.

CREON With a just quarrel weakness conquers might.

OEDIPUS Ye hear his words?

CHORUS   Aye words, but not yet deeds, Zeus knoweth!

CREON   Zeus may haply know, not thou.

CHORUS Insolence!

CREON   Insolence that thou must bear.

CHORUS   Haste ye princes, sound the alarm! Men of Athens, arm ye, arm!   Quickly to the rescue come Ere the robbers get them home. [Enter THESEUS]

THESEUS Why this outcry? What is forward? wherefore was I called away From the altar of Poseidon, lord of your Colonus? Say! On what errand have I hurried hither without stop or stay.

OEDIPUS Dear friend--those accents tell me who thou art-- Yon man but now hath done me a foul wrong.

THESEUS What is this wrong and who hath wrought it? Speak.

OEDIPUS Creon who stands before thee. He it is Hath robbed

me of my all, my daughters twain.

THESEUS What means this?

OEDIPUS Thou hast heard my tale of wrongs.

THESEUS Ho! hasten to the altars, one of you. Command my liegemen leave the sacrifice And hurry, foot and horse, with rein unchecked, To where the paths that packmen use diverge, Lest the two maidens slip away, and I Become a mockery to this my guest, As one despoiled by force. Quick, as I bid. As for this stranger, had I let my rage, Justly provoked, have play, he had not 'scaped Scathless and uncorrected at my hands. But now the laws to which himself appealed, These and none others shall adjudicate. Thou shalt not quit this land, till thou hast fetched The maidens and produced them in my sight. Thou hast offended both against myself And thine own race and country. Having come Unto a State that champions right and asks For every action warranty of law, Thou hast set aside the custom of the land, And like some freebooter art carrying off What plunder pleases thee, as if forsooth Thou thoughtest this a city without men, Or manned by slaves, and me a thing of naught. Yet not from Thebes this villainy was learnt; Thebes is not wont to breed unrighteous sons, Nor would she praise thee, if she learnt that thou Wert robbing me--aye and the gods to boot, Haling by force their suppliants, poor maids. Were I on Theban soil, to prosecute The justest claim imaginable, I Would never wrest by violence my own Without sanction of your State or King; I should behave as fits an outlander Living amongst a foreign folk, but thou Shamest a city that deserves it not, Even thine own, and plenitude of years Have made of thee an old man and a fool. Therefore again I charge thee as before, See that the maidens are restored at once, Unless thou would'st continue here by force And not by choice a sojourner; so much I tell thee home and what I say, I mean.

CHORUS Thy case is perilous; though by birth and race Thou should'st be just, thou plainly doest wrong.

CREON Not deeming this city void of men Or counsel, son of Aegeus, as thou say'st I did what I have done; rather I thought Your people were not like to set such store by kin of mine and keep them 'gainst my will. Nor would they harbor, so I stood assured, A godless parricide, a reprobate Convicted of incestuous marriage ties. For on her native hill of Ares here (I knew your far-famed Areopagus) Sits Justice, and permits not vagrant folk To stay within your borders. In that faith I hunted down my quarry; and e'en then

I had refrained but for the curses dire Wherewith he banned my kinsfolk and myself: Such wrong, methought, had warrant for my act. Anger has no old age but only death; The dead alone can feel no touch of spite. So thou must work thy will; my cause is just But weak without allies; yet will I try, Old as I am, to answer deeds with deeds.

OEDIPUS O shameless railer, think'st thou this abuse Defames my grey hairs rather than thine own? Murder and incest, deeds of horror, all Thou blurtest forth against me, all I have borne, No willing sinner; so it pleased the gods Wrath haply with my sinful race of old, Since thou could'st find no sin in me myself For which in retribution I was doomed To trespass thus against myself and mine. Answer me now, if by some oracle My sire was destined to a bloody end By a son's hand, can this reflect on me, Me then unborn, begotten by no sire, Conceived in no mother's womb? And if When born to misery, as born I was, I met my sire, not knowing whom I met or what I did, and slew him, how canst thou With justice blame the all-unconscious hand? And for my mother, wretch, art not ashamed, Seeing she was thy sister, to extort From me the story of her marriage, such A marriage as I straightway will proclaim. For I will speak; thy lewd and impious speech Has broken all the bonds of reticence. She was, ah woe is me! she was my mother; I knew it not, nor she; and she my mother Bare children to the son whom she had borne, A birth of shame. But this at least I know Wittingly thou aspersest her and me; But I unwitting wed, unwilling speak. Nay neither in this marriage or this deed Which thou art ever casting in my teeth-- A murdered sire--shall I be held to blame. Come, answer me one question, if thou canst: If one should presently attempt thy life, Would'st thou, O man of justice, first inquire If the assassin was perchance thy sire, Or turn upon him? As thou lov'st thy life, On thy aggressor thou would'st turn, no stay Debating, if the law would bear thee out. Such was my case, and such the pass whereto The gods reduced me; and methinks my sire, Could he come back to life, would not dissent. Yet thou, for just thou art not, but a man Who sticks at nothing, if it serve his plea, Reproachest me with this before these men. It serves thy turn to laud great Theseus' name, And Athens as a wisely governed State; Yet in thy flatteries one thing is to seek: If any land knows how to pay the gods Their proper rites, 'tis Athens most of all. This is the land whence thou wast fain to steal Their aged suppliant and hast carried off My daughters. Therefore to yon goddesses, I turn, adjure them and invoke their aid To champion my cause, that thou mayest learn What is the breed of men who guard this State.

CHORUS An honest man, my liege, one sore bestead By fortune, and so worthy our support.

THESEUS Enough of words; the captors speed amain, While we the victims stand debating here.

CREON What would'st thou? What can I, a feeble man?

THESEUS Show us the trail, and I'll attend thee too, That, if thou hast the maidens hereabouts, Thou mayest thyself discover them to me; But if thy guards outstrip us with their spoil, We may draw rein; for others speed, from whom They will not 'scape to thank the gods at home. Lead on, I say, the captor's caught, and fate Hath ta'en the fowler in the toils he spread; So soon are lost gains gotten by deceit. And look not for allies; I know indeed Such height of insolence was never reached Without abettors or accomplices; Thou hast some backer in thy bold essay, But I will search this matter home and see One man doth not prevail against the State. Dost take my drift, or seem these words as vain As seemed our warnings when the plot was hatched?

CREON Nothing thou sayest can I here dispute, But once at home I too shall act my part.

THESEUS Threaten us and--begone! Thou, Oedipus, Stay here assured that nothing save my death Will stay my purpose to restore the maids.

OEDIPUS Heaven bless thee, Theseus, for thy nobleness And all thy loving care in my behalf. [Exeunt THESEUS and CREON]

CHORUS (Str. 1) O when the flying foe, Turning at last to bay, Soon will give blow for blow, Might I behold the fray; Hear the loud battle roar Swell, on the Pythian shore, Or by the torch-lit bay, Where the dread Queen and Maid Cherish the mystic rites, Rites they to none betray, Ere on his lips is laid Secrecy's golden key By their own acolytes,   Priestly Eumolpidae.

There I might chance behold Theseus our captain bold Meet with the robber band, Ere they have fled the land, Rescue by might and main Maidens, the captives twain.

(Ant. 1) Haply on swiftest steed, Or in the flying car, Now they approach the glen, West of white Oea's scaur. They will be vanquished: Dread are our warriors, dread Theseus our chieftain's men. Flashes each bridle bright,

Charges each gallant knight, All that our Queen adore,
Pallas their patron, or Him whose wide floods enring Earth,   the
great Ocean-king Whom Rhea bore.

(Str. 2) Fight they or now prepare To fight? a vision rare
Tells me that soon again I shall behold the twain Maidens so ill
bestead, By their kin buffeted. Today, today Zeus worketh some
great thing This day shall victory bring. O for the wings, the wings
of a dove, To be borne with the speed of the gale, Up and still up-
wards to sail   And gaze on the fray from the clouds above. (Ant.
2) All-seeing Zeus, O lord of heaven, To our guardian host be giv-
en Might triumphant to surprise Flying foes and win their prize.
Hear us, Zeus, and hear us, child Of Zeus, Athene undefiled, Hear,
Apollo, hunter, hear, Huntress, sister of Apollo, Who the dappled
swift-foot deer O'er the wooded glade dost follow; Help with your
two-fold power Athens in danger's hour! O wayfarer, thou wilt not
have to tax The friends who watch for thee with false presage, For
lo, an escort with the maids draws near. [Enter ANTIGONE and
ISMENE with THESEUS]

OEDIPUS Where, where? what sayest thou?

ANTIGONE O father, father, Would that some god might grant
thee eyes to see This best of men who brings us back again.

OEDIPUS My child! and are ye back indeed!

ANTIGONE Yes, saved By Theseus and his gallant followers.

OEDIPUS Come to your father's arms, O let me feel A child's
embrace I never hoped for more.

ANTIGONE Thou askest what is doubly sweet to give.

OEDIPUS Where are ye then?

ANTIGONE We come together both.

OEDIPUS My precious nurslings!

ANTIGONE Fathers aye were fond.

OEDIPUS Props of my age!

ANTIGONE So sorrow sorrow props.

OEDIPUS I have my darlings, and if death should come, Death
were not wholly bitter with you near. Cling to me, press me close

on either side, There rest ye from your dreary wayfaring. Now tell me of your ventures, but in brief; Brief speech suffices for young maids like you.

ANTIGONE Here is our savior; thou should'st hear the tale From his own lips; so shall my part be brief.

OEDIPUS I pray thee do not wonder if the sight Of children, given o'er for lost, has made My converse somewhat long and tedious. Full well I know the joy I have of them Is due to thee, to thee and no man else; Thou wast their sole deliverer, none else. The gods deal with thee after my desire, With thee and with this land! for fear of heaven I found above all peoples most with you, And righteousness and lips that cannot lie. I speak in gratitude of what I know, For all I have I owe to thee alone. Give me thy hand, O Prince, that I may touch it, And if thou wilt permit me, kiss thy cheek. What say I? Can I wish that thou should'st touch One fallen like me to utter wretchedness, Corrupt and tainted with a thousand ills? Oh no, I would not let thee if thou would'st. They only who have known calamity Can share it. Let me greet thee where thou art, And still befriend me as thou hast till now.

THESEUS I marvel not if thou hast dallied long In converse with thy children and preferred Their speech to mine; I feel no jealousy, I would be famous more by deeds than words. Of this, old friend, thou hast had proof; my oath I have fulfilled and brought thee back the maids Alive and nothing harmed for all those threats. And how the fight was won, 'twere waste of words To boast--thy daughters here will tell thee all. But of a matter that has lately chanced On my way hitherward, I fain would have Thy counsel--slight 'twould seem, yet worthy thought. A wise man heeds all matters great or small.

OEDIPUS What is it, son of Aegeus? Let me hear. Of what thou askest I myself know naught.

THESEUS 'Tis said a man, no countryman of thine, But of thy kin, hath taken sanctuary Beside the altar of Poseidon, where I was at sacrifice when called away.

OEDIPUS What is his country? what the suitor's prayer?

THESEUS I know but one thing; he implores, I am told, A word with thee--he will not trouble thee.

OEDIPUS What seeks he? If a suppliant, something grave.

THESEUS He only waits, they say, to speak with thee, And then unharmed to go upon his way.

OEDIPUS I marvel who is this petitioner.

THESEUS Think if there be not any of thy kin At Argos who might claim this boon of thee.

OEDIPUS Dear friend, forbear, I pray.

THESEUS What ails thee now?

OEDIPUS Ask it not of me.

THESEUS Ask not what? explain.

OEDIPUS Thy words have told me who the suppliant is.

THESEUS Who can he be that I should frown on him?

OEDIPUS My son, O king, my hateful son, whose words Of all men's most would jar upon my ears.

THESEUS Thou sure mightest listen. If his suit offend, No need to grant it. Why so loth to hear him?

OEDIPUS That voice, O king, grates on a father's ears; I have come to loathe it. Force me not to yield.

THESEUS But he hath found asylum. O beware, And fail not in due reverence to the god.

ANTIGONE O heed me, father, though I am young in years. Let the prince have his will and pay withal What in his eyes is service to the god; For our sake also let our brother come. If what he urges tend not to thy good He cannot surely wrest perforce thy will. To hear him then, what harm? By open words A scheme of villainy is soon bewrayed. Thou art his father, therefore canst not pay In kind a son's most impious outrages. O listen to him; other men like thee Have thankless children and are choleric, But yielding to persuasion's gentle spell They let their savage mood be exorcised. Look thou to the past, forget the present, think On all the woe thy sire and mother brought thee; Thence wilt thou draw this lesson without fail, Of evil passion evil is the end. Thou hast, alas, to prick thy memory, Stern monitors, these ever-sightless orbs. O yield to us; just suitors should not need To be importunate, nor he that takes A favor lack the grace to make return.

OEDIPUS Grievous to me, my child, the boon ye win By pleading. Let it be then; have your way Only if come he must, I beg thee, friend, Let none have power to dispose of me.

THESEUS No need, Sir, to appeal a second time. It likes me not to boast, but be assured Thy life is safe while any god saves mine. [Exit THESEUS]

CHORUS (Str.) Who craves excess of days,Scorning the common span Of life, I judge that man A giddy wight who walks in folly's ways. For the long years heap up a grievous load, Scant pleasures, heavier pains, Till not one joy remains For him who lingers on life's weary road And come it slow or fast, One doom of fate   Doth all await, For dance and marriage bell,   The   dirge and funeral knell. Death the deliverer freeth all at last.

(Ant.) Not to be born at all Is best, far best that can befall, Next best, when born, with least delay To trace the backward way. For when youth passes with its giddy train, Troubles on troubles follow, toils on toils, Pain, pain for ever pain;   And   none   escapes life's coils. Envy, sedition, strife, Carnage and war, make up the tale of life. Last comes the worst and most abhorred stage Of unregarded age, Joyless, companionless and slow, Of woes the crowning woe.

(Epode) Such ills not I alone, He too our guest hath known, E'en as some headland on an iron-bound shore, Lashed by the wintry blasts and surge's roar, So is he buffeted on every side By drear misfortune's whelming tide, By every wind of heaven o'erborne Some from the sunset, some from orient morn, Some   from   the noonday glow. Some from Rhipean gloom of everlasting snow.

ANTIGONE Father, methinks I see the stranger coming, Alone he comes and weeping plenteous tears.

OEDIPUS Who may he be?

ANTIGONE The same that we surmised. From the outset-- Polyneices. He is here. [Enter POLYNEICES]

POLYNEICES Ah me, my sisters, shall I first lament My own afflictions, or my aged sire's, Whom here I find a castaway, with you, In a strange land, an ancient beggar clad In antic tatters, marring all his frame, While o'er the sightless orbs his unkept locks Float in the breeze; and, as it were to match, He bears a wallet against hunger's pinch. All this too late I learn, wretch that I am,

Alas! I own it, and am proved most vile In my neglect of thee: I scorn myself. But as almighty Zeus in all he doth Hath Mercy for co-partner of this throne, Let Mercy, father, also sit enthroned In thy heart likewise. For transgressions past May be amended, cannot be made worse.

Why silent? Father, speak, nor turn away, Hast thou no word, wilt thou dismiss me then In mute disdain, nor tell me why thou art wrath? O ye his daughters, sisters mine, do ye This sullen, obstinate silence try to move. Let him not spurn, without a single word Of answer, me the suppliant of the god.

ANTIGONE Tell him thyself, unhappy one, thine errand; For large discourse may send a thrill of joy, Or stir a chord of wrath or tenderness, And to the tongue-tied somehow give a tongue.

POLYNEICES Well dost thou counsel, and I will speak out. First will I call in aid the god himself, Poseidon, from whose altar I was raised, With warrant from the monarch of this land, To parley with you, and depart unscathed. These pledges, strangers, I would see observed By you and by my sisters and my sire. Now, father, let me tell thee why I came. I have been banished from my native land Because by right of primogeniture I claimed possession of thy sovereign throne Wherefrom Etocles, my younger brother, Ousted me, not by weight of precedent, Nor by the last arbitrament of war, But by his popular acts; and the prime cause Of this I deem the curse that rests on thee. So likewise hold the soothsayers, for when I came to Argos in the Dorian land And took the king Adrastus' child to wife, Under my standard I enlisted all The foremost captains of the Apian isle, To levy with their aid that sevenfold host Of spearmen against Thebes, determining To oust my foes or die in a just cause. Why then, thou askest, am I here today? Father, I come a suppliant to thee Both for myself and my allies who now With squadrons seven beneath their seven spears Beleaguer all the plain that circles Thebes. Foremost the peerless warrior, peerless seer, Amphiaraiis with his lightning lance; Next an Aetolian, Tydeus, Oeneus' son; Eteoclus of Argive birth the third; The fourth Hippomedon, sent to the war By his sire Talaos; Capaneus, the fifth, Vaunts he will fire and raze the town; the sixth Parthenopaeus, an Arcadian born Named of that maid, longtime a maid and late Espoused, Atalanta's true-born child; Last I thy son, or thine at least in name, If but the bastard of an evil fate, Lead against Thebes the fearless Argive host. Thus by thy children and thy life, my sire, We all adjure thee to remit thy wrath And favor one who seeks a just revenge Against a brother who has banned and robbed him. For victory, if oracles speak true, Will fall to those who have thee for ally. So, by our fountains and familiar gods I pray thee, yield and hear; a beggar I And exile, thou an exile likewise; both Involved in one misfortune find a home As pensioners, while he, the lord of Thebes, O agony! makes a mock of thee and me. I'll scatter with a breath the upstart's might, And bring thee home again and stablish thee, And stablish, having cast him out, myself. This will thy goodwill I will undertake, Without it I can scare return alive.

CHORUS For the king's sake who sent him, Oedipus, Dismiss him not without a meet reply.

OEDIPUS Nay, worthy seniors, but for Theseus' sake Who sent him hither to have word of me. Never again would he have heard my voice; But now he shall obtain this parting grace, An answer that will bring him little joy. O villain, when thou hadst the sovereignty That now thy brother holdeth in thy stead, Didst thou not drive me, thine own father, out, An exile, cityless, and make we wear This beggar's garb thou weepest to behold, Now thou art come thyself to my sad plight? Nothing is here for tears; it must be borne By me till death, and I shall think of thee As of my murderer; thou didst thrust me out; 'Tis thou hast made me conversant with woe, Through thee I beg my bread in a strange land; And had not these my daughters tended me I had been dead for aught of aid from thee. They tend me, they preserve me, they are men Not women in true service to their sire; But ye are bastards, and no sons of mine. Therefore just Heaven hath an eye on thee; Howbeit not yet with aspect so austere As thou shalt soon experience, if indeed These banded hosts are moving against Thebes. That city thou canst never storm, but first Shall fall, thou and thy brother, blood-imbrued. Such curse I lately launched against you twain, Such curse I now invoke to fight for me, That ye may learn to honor those who bear thee Nor flout a sightless father who begat Degenerate sons--these maidens did not so. Therefore my curse is stronger than thy "throne," Thy "suppliance," if by right of laws eterne Primeval Justice sits enthroned with Zeus. Begone, abhorred, disowned, no son of mine, Thou vilest of the vile! and take with thee This curse I leave thee as my last bequest:-- Never to win by arms thy native land, No, nor return to Argos in the Vale, But by a kinsman's hand to die and slay Him who expelled thee. So I pray and call On the ancestral gloom of Tartarus To snatch thee hence, on these dread goddesses I call, and Ares who incensed you both To mortal enmity. Go now proclaim What thou hast heard to the Cadmeians all, Thy staunch confederates--this the heritage that Oedipus divideth to his sons.

CHORUS Thy errand, Polyneices, liked me not From the beginning; now go back with speed.

POLYNEICES Woe worth my journey and my baffled hopes! Woe worth my comrades! What a desperate end To that glad march from Argos! Woe is me! I dare not whisper it to my allies Or turn them back, but mute must meet my doom. My sisters, ye his daughters, ye have heard The prayers of our stern father, if his curse Should come to pass and ye some day return To Thebes, O then disown me not, I pray, But grant me burial and due funeral rites. So shall the praise your filial care now wins Be doubled for the service wrought for me.

ANTIGONE One boon, O Polyneices, let me crave.

POLYNEICES What would'st thou, sweet Antigone? Say on.

ANTIGONE Turn back thy host to Argos with all speed, And ruin not thyself and Thebes as well.

POLYNEICES That cannot be. How could I lead again An army that had seen their leader quail?

ANTIGONE But, brother, why shouldst thou be wroth again? What profit from thy country's ruin comes?

POLYNEICES 'Tis shame to live in exile, and shall I The elder bear a younger brother's flouts?

ANTIGONE Wilt thou then bring to pass his prophecies Who threatens mutual slaughter to you both?

POLYNEICES Aye, so he wishes:--but I must not yield.

ANTIGONE O woe is me! but say, will any dare, Hearing his prophecy, to follow thee?

POLYNEICES I shall not tell it; a good general Reports successes and conceals mishaps.

ANTIGONE Misguided youth, thy purpose then stands fast!

POLYNEICES 'Tis so, and stay me not. The road I choose, Dogged by my sire and his avenging spirit, Leads me to ruin; but for you may Zeus Make your path bright if ye fulfill my hest When dead; in life ye cannot serve me more. Now let me go, farewell, a long farewell! Ye ne'er shall see my living face again.

ANTIGONE Ah me!

POLYNEICES Bewail me not.

ANTIGONE Who would not mourn Thee, brother, hurrying to an open pit!

POLYNEICES If I must die, I must.

ANTIGONE Nay, hear me plead.

POLYNEICES It may not be; forbear.

ANTIGONE Then woe is me, If I must lose thee.

POLYNEICES Nay, that rests with fate, Whether I live or die; but for you both I pray to heaven ye may escape all ill; For ye are blameless in the eyes of all. [Exit POLYNEICES]

CHORUS (Str. 1) Ills on ills! no pause or rest! Come they from our sightless guest? Or haply now we see fulfilled What fate long time hath willed? For ne'er have I proved vain Aught   that   the heavenly powers ordain. Time with never sleeping eye W a t c h e s what is writ on high, Overthrowing now the great, Raising now from low estate. Hark! How the thunder rumbles! Zeus defend us!

OEDIPUS Children, my children! will no messenger Go summon hither Theseus my best friend?

ANTIGONE And wherefore, father, dost thou summon him?

OEDIPUS This winged thunder of the god must bear me Anon to Hades. Send and tarry not.

CHORUS (Ant. 1) Hark! with louder, nearer roar The bolt of Zeus descends once more. My spirit quails and cowers: my hair Bristles for fear. Again that flare! What doth the lightning-flash portend? Ever it points to issues grave. Dread powers of air! Save, Zeus, O save!

OEDIPUS Daughters, upon me the predestined end Has come; no turning from it any more.

ANTIGONE How knowest thou? What sign convinces thee?

OEDIPUS I know full well. Let some one with all speed Go summon hither the Athenian prince.

CHORUS (Str. 2) Ha! once more the deafening sound Peals yet louder all around If thou darkenest our land, Lightly, lightly lay thy hand; Grace, not anger, let me win, If upon a man of sin I have looked with pitying eye, Zeus, our king, to thee I cry!

OEDIPUS Is the prince coming? Will he when he comes Find me yet living and my senses clear!

ANTIGONE What solemn charge would'st thou impress on him?

OEDIPUS For all his benefits I would perform The promise made when I received them first.

CHORUS (Ant. 2) Hither haste, my son, arise, Altar leave and sacrifice, If haply to Poseidon now In the far glade thou pay'st thy vow. For our guest to thee would bring And thy folk and offering, Thy due guerdon. Haste, O King! [Enter THESEUS]

THESEUS Wherefore again this general din? at once My people call me and the stranger calls. Is it a thunderbolt of Zeus or sleet Of arrowy hail? a storm so fierce as this Would warrant all surmises of mischance.

OEDIPUS Thou com'st much wished for, Prince, and sure some god Hath bid good luck attend thee on thy way.

THESEUS What, son of Laius, hath chanced of new?

OEDIPUS My life hath turned the scale. I would do all I promised thee and thine before I die.

THESEUS What sign assures thee that thine end is near?

OEDIPUS The gods themselves are heralds of my fate; Of their appointed warnings nothing fails.

THESEUS How sayest thou they signify their will?

OEDIPUS This thunder, peal on peal, this lightning hurled Flash upon flash, from the unconquered hand.

THESEUS I must believe thee, having found thee oft A prophet true; then speak what must be done.

OEDIPUS O son of Aegeus, for this state will I Unfold a treasure age cannot corrupt. Myself anon without a guiding hand Will take thee to the spot where I must end. This secret ne'er reveal to mortal man, Neither the spot nor whereabouts it lies, So shall it ever serve thee for defense Better than native shields and near allies. But those dread mysteries speech may not profane Thyself shalt gather coming there alone; Since not to any of thy subjects, nor To my own children, though I love them dearly, Can I reveal what thou must guard alone, And whisper to thy chosen heir alone, So to be handed down from heir to heir. Thus shalt thou hold this land inviolate From the dread Dragon's brood. [7] The justest State By countless wanton neighbors may be wronged, For the gods, though they tarry, mark for doom The godless sinner in his mad career. Far from thee, son of Aegeus, be such fate! But to the spot--the god within me goads-- Let us set forth no longer hesitate. Follow me, daughters, this way. Strange that I Whom you have led so long should lead you now. Oh, touch me not, but let me all alone Find out the sepulcher that destiny Appoints me in this land. Hither, this way, For this way Hermes leads, the spirit guide, And Persephassa, empress of the dead. O light, no light to me, but mine erewhile, Now the last time I feel thee palpable, For I am drawing near the final gloom Of Hades. Blessing on thee, dearest friend, On thee and on thy land and followers! Live prosperous and in your happy state Still for your welfare think on me, the dead. [Exit THESEUS followed by ANTIGONE and ISMENE]

CHORUS (Str.) If mortal prayers are heard in hell, Hear, Goddess dread, invisible! Monarch of the regions drear, Aidoneus, hear, O hear! By a gentle, tearless doom Speed this stranger to the gloom, Let him enter without pain The all-shrouding Stygian plain. Wrongfully in life oppressed, Be he now by Justice blessed.

(Ant.) Queen infernal, and thou fell Watch-dog of the gates of hell, Who, as legends tell, dost glare, Gnarling in thy cavernous lair At all comers, let him go Scathless to the fields below. For thy master orders thus, The son of earth and Tartarus; In his den the monster keep, Giver of eternal sleep. [Enter MESSENGER]

MESSENGER Friends, countrymen, my tidings are in sum That Oedipus is gone, but the event Was not so brief, nor can the tale be brief.

CHORUS What, has he gone, the unhappy man?

MESSENGER Know well That he has passed away from life to death.

CHORUS How? By a god-sent, painless doom, poor soul?

MESSENGER Thy question hits the marvel of the tale. How he moved hence, you saw him and must know; Without a friend to lead the way, himself Guiding us all. So having reached the abrupt Earth-rooted Threshold with its brazen stairs, He paused at one of the converging paths, Hard by the rocky basin which records The pact of Theseus and Peirithous. Betwixt that rift and the Thorician rock, The hollow pear-tree and the marble tomb, Midway he sat and loosed his beggar's weeds; Then calling to his daughters bade them fetch Of running water, both to wash withal And make libation; so they clomb the steep; And in brief space brought what their father bade, Then laved and dressed him with observance due. But when he had his will in everything, And no desire was left unsatisfied, It thundered from the netherworld; the maids Shivered, and crouching at their father's knees Wept, beat their breast and uttered a long wail. He, as he heard their sudden bitter cry, Folded his arms about them both and said, "My children, ye will lose your sire today, For all of me has perished, and no more Have ye to bear your long, long ministry; A heavy load, I know, and yet one word Wipes out all score of tribulations--love. And love from me ye had--from no man more; But now must live without me all your days." So clinging to each other sobbed and wept Father and daughters both, but when at last Their mourning had an end and no wail rose, A moment there was silence; suddenly A voice that summoned him; with sudden dread The hair of all stood up and all were 'mazed; For the call came, now loud, now low, and oft. "Oedipus, Oedipus, why tarry we? Too long, too long thy passing is delayed." But when he heard the summons of the god, He prayed that Theseus might be brought, and when The Prince came nearer: "O my friend," he cried, "Pledge ye my daughters, giving thy right hand-- And, daughters, give him yours--and promise me Thou never wilt forsake them, but do all That time and friendship prompt in their behoof." And he of his nobility repressed His tears and swore to be their constant friend. This promise given, Oedipus put forth Blind hands and laid them on his children, saying, "O children, prove your true nobility And hence depart nor seek to witness sights Unlawful or to hear unlawful words. Nay, go with speed; let none but Theseus stay, Our ruler, to behold what next shall hap." So we all heard him speak, and weeping sore We companied the maidens on their way. After brief space we looked again, and lo The man was gone, evanished from our eyes; Only the king we saw with upraised hand Shading his eyes as from some awful sight, That no man might endure to look upon. A moment later, and we saw him bend In prayer to Earth and prayer to Heaven at once. But by what doom the stranger met his end No man save Theseus knoweth. For there fell No fiery bold that reft him in that hour, Nor whirlwind from the sea, but he was taken. It was a messenger from heaven, or else Some gentle, painless cleaving of earth's base; For without wailing or disease or pain He passed away--and end most marvelous. And if to some my tale seems foolishness I am content that such could count me fool.

CHORUS Where are the maids and their attendant friends?

MESSENGER They cannot be far off; the approaching sound Of lamentation tells they come this way. [Enter ANTIGONE and ISMENE]

ANTIGONE (Str. 1) Woe, woe! on this sad day We sisters of one blasted stock must bow beneath the shock, Must weep and weep the curse that lay On him our sire, for whom In life, a life-long world of care 'Twas ours to bear, In death must face the gloom That wraps his tomb. What tongue can tell That sight ineffable?

CHORUS What mean ye, maidens?

ANTIGONE All is but surmise.

CHORUS Is he then gone?

ANTIGONE Gone as ye most might wish. Not in battle or sea storm, But reft from sight, By hands invisible borne To viewless fields of night. Ah me! on us too night has come, The night of mourning. Wither roam O'er land or sea in our distress Eating the bread of bitterness?

ISMENE I know not. O that Death Might nip my breath, And let me share my aged father's fate. I cannot live a life thus desolate.

CHORUS Best of daughters, worthy pair, What heaven brings ye needs must bear, Fret no more 'gainst Heaven's will; Fate hath dealt with you not ill.

ANTIGONE (Ant. 1) Love can turn past pain to bliss, What seemed bitter now is sweet. Ah me! that happy toil is sweet.

The guidance of those dear blind feet. Dear father, wrapt for aye in nether gloom, E'en in the tomb Never shalt thou lack of love repine, Her love and mine.

CHORUS His fate--

ANTIGONE Is even as he planned.

CHORUS How so?

ANTIGONE He died, so willed he, in a foreign land. Lapped in kind earth he sleeps his long last sleep, And o'er his grave friends weep. How great our lost these streaming eyes can tell, This sorrow naught can quell. Thou hadst thy wish 'mid strangers thus to die, But I, ah me, not by.

ISMENE Alas, my sister, what new fate Befalls us orphans desolate?

CHORUS His end was blessed; therefore, children, stay Your sorrow. Man is born to fate a prey.

ANTIGONE (Str. 2) Sister, let us back again.

ISMENE Why return?

ANTIGONE   My soul is fain-- ISMENE Is fain?

ANTIGONE   To see the earthy bed.

ISMENE Sayest thou?

ANTIGONE   Where our sire is laid.

ISMENE Nay, thou can'st not, dost not see--

ANTIGONE Sister, wherefore wroth with me?

ISMENE Know'st not--beside--

ANTIGONE   More must I hear?

ISMENE Tombless he died, none near.

ANTIGONE Lead me thither; slay me there.

ISMENE How shall I unhappy fare, Friendless, helpless, how drag on A life of misery alone?

CHORUS (Ant. 2) Fear not, maids--

ANTIGONE Ah, whither flee?

CHORUS Refuge hath been found.

ANTIGONE For me?

CHORUS Where thou shalt be safe from harm.

ANTIGONE I know it.

CHORUS Why then this alarm?

ANTIGONE How again to get us home I know not.

CHORUS Why then this roam?

ANTIGONE Troubles whelm us--

CHORUS As of yore.

ANTIGONE Worse than what was worse before.

CHORUS Sure ye are driven on the breakers' surge.

ANTIGONE Alas! we are.

CHORUS Alas! 'tis so.

ANTIGONE Ah whither turn, O Zeus? No ray Of hope to cheer the way Whereon the fates our desperate voyage urge. [Enter THESEUS]

THESEUS Dry your tears; when grace is shed On the quick and on the dead By dark Powers beneficent, Over-grief they would resent.

ANTIGONE Aegeus' child, to thee we pray.

THESEUS What the boon, my children, say.

ANTIGONE With our own eyes we fain would see Our father's tomb.

THESEUS That may not be.

ANTIGONE What say'st thou, King?

THESEUS My children, he Charged me straitly that no moral Should approach the sacred portal, Or greet with funeral litanies The hidden tomb wherein he lies; Saying, "If thou keep'st my hest Thou shalt hold thy realm at rest." The God of Oaths this promise heard, And to Zeus I pledged my word.

ANTIGONE Well, if he would have it so, We must yield. Then let us go Back to Thebes, if yet we may Heal this mortal feud and stay The self-wrought doom That drives our brothers to their tomb.

THESEUS Go in peace; nor will I spare Ought of toil and zealous care, But on all your needs attend, Gladdening in his grave my friend.

CHORUS Wail no more, let sorrow rest, All is ordered for the best.

FOOTNOTES ---------

[Footnote 4: The Greek text for the passages marked here and later in the text have been lost.]

[Footnote 5: To avoid the blessing, still a secret, he resorts to   a commonplace; literally, "For what generous man is not (in befriending others) a friend to himself?"]

[Footnote 6: Creon desires to bury Oedipus on the confines of Thebes so as to avoid the pollution and yet offer due rites at his tomb. Ismene tells him of the latest oracle and interprets to him its purport, that some day the Theban invaders of Athens will be routed in a battle near the grave of Oedipus.]

[Footnote 7: The Thebans sprung from the Dragon's teeth sown by Cadmus.]

ANTIGONE

ARGUMENT

Antigone, daughter of Oedipus, the late king of Thebes, in defiance of Creon who rules in his stead, resolves to bury her brother Polyneices, slain in his attack on Thebes. She is caught in the act by Creon's watchmen and brought before the king. She justifies her action, asserting that she was bound to obey the eternal laws of right and wrong in spite of any human ordinance. Creon, unrelenting, condemns her to be immured in a rock-hewn chamber. His son Haemon, to whom Antigone is betrothed, pleads in vain for her life and threatens to die with her. Warned by the seer Teiresias Creon repents him and hurries to release Antigone from her rocky prison. But he is too late: he finds lying side by side Antigone who had hanged herself and Haemon who also has perished by his own hand. Returning to the palace he sees within the dead body of his queen who on learning of her son's death has stabbed herself to the heart.

DRAMATIS PERSONAE

ANTIGONE and ISMENE--daughters of Oedipus and sisters of Polyneices and Eteocles.

CREON, King of Thebes.

HAEMON, Son of Creon, betrothed to Antigone.

EURYDICE, wife of Creon.

TEIRESIAS, the prophet.

CHORUS, of Theban elders.

A WATCHMAN

A MESSENGER

A SECOND MESSENGER

ANTIGONE

ANTIGONE and ISMENE before the Palace gates.

ANTIGONE Ismene, sister of my blood and heart, See'st thou how Zeus would in our lives fulfill The weird of Oedipus, a world of woes! For what of pain, affliction, outrage, shame, Is lacking in our fortunes, thine and mine? And now this proclamation of today Made by our Captain-General to the State, What can its purport be? Didst hear and heed, Or art thou deaf when friends are banned as foes?

ISMENE To me, Antigone, no word of friends Has come, or glad or grievous, since we twain Were reft of our two brethren in one day By double fratricide; and since i' the night Our Argive leaguers fled, no later news Has reached me, to inspirit or deject.

ANTIGONE I know 'twas so, and therefore summoned thee Beyond the gates to breathe it in thine ear.

ISMENE What is it? Some dark secret stirs thy breast.

ANTIGONE What but the thought of our two brothers dead, The one by Creon graced with funeral rites, The other disappointed? Eteocles He hath consigned to earth (as fame reports) With obsequies that use and wont ordain, So gracing him among the dead below. But Polyneices, a dishonored corse, (So by report the royal edict runs) No man may bury him or make lament-- Must leave him tombless and unwept, a feast For kites to scent afar and swoop upon. Such is the edict (if report speak true) Of Creon, our most noble Creon, aimed At thee and me, aye me too; and anon He will be here to promulgate, for such As have not heard, his mandate; 'tis in sooth No passing humor, for the edict says Whoe'er transgresses shall be stoned to death. So stands it with us; now 'tis thine to show If thou art worthy of thy blood or base.

ISMENE But how, my rash, fond sister, in such case Can I do anything to make or mar?

ANTIGONE Say, wilt thou aid me and abet? Decide.

ISMENE In what bold venture? What is in thy thought?

ANTIGONE Lend me a hand to bear the corpse away.

ISMENE What, bury him despite the interdict?

ANTIGONE My brother, and, though thou deny him, thine No man shall say that I betrayed a brother.

ISMENE Wilt thou persist, though Creon has forbid?

ANTIGONE What right has he to keep me from my own?

ISMENE Bethink thee, sister, of our father's fate, Abhorred, dishonored, self-convinced of sin, Blinded, himself his executioner. Think of his mother-wife (ill sorted names) Done by a noose herself had twined to death And last, our hapless brethren in one day, Both in a mutual destiny involved, Self-slaughtered, both the slayer and the slain. Bethink thee, sister, we are left alone; Shall we not perish wretchedest of all, If in defiance of the law we cross A monarch's will?--weak women, think of that, Not framed by nature to contend with men. Remember this too that the stronger rules; We must obey his orders, these or worse. Therefore I plead compulsion and entreat The dead to pardon. I perforce obey The powers that be. 'Tis foolishness, I ween, To overstep in aught the golden mean.

ANTIGONE I urge no more; nay, wert thou willing still, I would not welcome such a fellowship. Go thine own way; myself will bury him. How sweet to die in such employ, to rest,-- Sister and brother linked in love's embrace-- A sinless sinner, banned awhile on earth, But by the dead commended; and with them I shall abide for ever. As for thee, Scorn, if thou wilt, the eternal laws of Heaven.

ISMENE I scorn them not, but to defy the State Or break her ordinance I have no skill.

ANTIGONE A specious pretext. I will go alone To lap my dearest brother in the grave.

ISMENE My poor, fond sister, how I fear for thee!

ANTIGONE O waste no fears on me; look to thyself.

ISMENE At least let no man know of thine intent, But keep it close and secret, as will I.

ANTIGONE O tell it, sister; I shall hate thee more If thou proclaim it not to all the town.

ISMENE Thou hast a fiery soul for numbing work.

ANTIGONE I pleasure those whom I would liefest please.

ISMENE If thou succeed; but thou art doomed to fail.

ANTIGONE When strength shall fail me, yes, but not before.

ISMENE But, if the venture's hopeless, why essay?

ANTIGONE Sister, forbear, or I shall hate thee soon, And the dead man will hate thee too, with cause. Say I am mad and give my madness rein To wreck itself; the worst that can befall Is but to die an honorable death.

ISMENE Have thine own way then; 'tis a mad endeavor, Yet to thy lovers thou art dear as ever. [Exeunt]

CHORUS (Str. 1) Sunbeam, of all that ever dawn upon Our seven-gated Thebes the brightest ray, O eye of golden day, How fair thy light o'er Dirce's fountain shone, Speeding upon their headlong homeward course, Far quicker than they came, the Argive force; Putting to flight The argent shields, the host with scutcheons white. Against our land the proud invader came To vindicate fell Polyneices' claim. Like to an eagle swooping low, O n pinions white as new fall'n snow. With clanging scream, a horsetail plume his crest, The aspiring lord of Argos onward pressed.

(Ant. 1) Hovering around our city walls he waits, His spearmen raven at our seven gates. But ere a torch our crown of towers could burn, Ere they had tasted of our blood, they turn Forced by the Dragon; in their rear The din of Ares panic-struck they hear. For Zeus who hates the braggart's boast Beheld that gold-bespangled host; As at the goal the paean they upraise, He struck them with his forked lightning blaze.

(Str. 2) To earthy from earth rebounding, down he crashed; The fire-brand from his impious hand was dashed, As like a Bacchic reveler on he came, Outbreathing hate and flame, And tottered. Elsewhere in the field, Here, there, great Area like a warhorse wheeled; Beneath his car down thrust Our foemen bit the dust.

Seven captains at our seven gates Thundered; for each a champion waits, Each left behind his armor bright, Trophy for Zeus who turns the fight; Save two alone, that ill-starred pair One mother to one father bare, Who lance in rest, one 'gainst the other Drave, and both perished, brother slain by brother.

(Ant. 2) Now Victory to Thebes returns again And smiles upon her chariot-circled plain. Now let feast and festal should Memories of war blot out. Let us to the temples throng, Dance and sing the live night long. God of Thebes, lead thou the round. Bacchus, shaker of the ground! Let us end our revels here; Lo! Creon our new lord draws near, Crowned by this strange chance, our king. What, I marvel, pondering? Why this summons? Wherefore call Us, his elders, one and all, Bidding us with him debate, On some grave concern of State? [Enter CREON]

CREON Elders, the gods have righted one again Our storm-tossed ship of state, now safe in port. But you by special summons I convened As my most trusted councilors; first, because I knew you loyal to Laius of old; Again, when Oedipus restored our State, Both while he ruled and when his rule was o'er, Ye still were constant to the royal line. Now that his two sons perished in one day, Brother by brother murderously slain, By right of kinship to the Princes dead, I claim and hold the throne and sovereignty. Yet 'tis no easy matter to discern The temper of a man, his mind and will, Till he be proved by exercise of power; And in my case, if one who reigns supreme Swerve from the highest policy, tongue-tied By fear of consequence, that man I hold, And ever held, the basest of the base. And I contemn the man who sets his friend Before his country. For myself, I call To witness Zeus, whose eyes are everywhere, If I perceive some mischievous design To sap the State, I will not hold my tongue; Nor would I reckon as my private friend A public foe, well knowing that the State Is the good ship that holds our fortunes all: Farewell to friendship, if she suffers wreck. Such is the policy by which I seek To serve the Commons and conformably I have proclaimed an edict as concerns The sons of Oedipus; Eteocles Who in his country's battle fought and fell, The foremost champion--duly bury him With all observances and ceremonies That are the guerdon of the heroic dead. But for the miscreant exile who returned Minded in flames and ashes to blot out His father's city and his father's gods, And glut his vengeance with his kinsmen's blood, Or drag them captive at his chariot wheels-- For Polyneices 'tis ordained that none Shall give him burial or make mourn for him, But leave his corpse unburied, to be meat For dogs and carrion crows, a ghastly sight. So am I purposed; never by my will Shall miscreants take precedence of true men, But all good patriots, alive or dead, Shall be by me preferred and honored.

CHORUS Son of Menoeceus, thus thou will'st to deal With him who loathed and him who loved our State. Thy word is law; thou canst dispose of us The living, as thou will'st, as of the dead.

CREON See then ye execute what I ordain.

CHORUS On younger shoulders lay this grievous charge.

CREON Fear not, I've posted guards to watch the corpse.

CHORUS What further duty would'st thou lay on us?

CREON Not to connive at disobedience.

CHORUS No man is mad enough to court his death.

CREON The penalty is death: yet hope of gain Hath lured men to their ruin oftentimes. [Enter GUARD]

GUARD My lord, I will not make pretense to pant And puff as some light-footed messenger. In sooth my soul beneath its pack of thought Made many a halt and turned and turned again; For conscience plied her spur and curb by turns. "Why hurry headlong to thy fate, poor fool?" She whispered. Then again, "If Creon learn This from another, thou wilt rue it worse." Thus leisurely I hastened on my road; Much thought extends a furlong to a league. But in the end the forward voice prevailed, To face thee. I will speak though I say nothing. For plucking courage from despair methought, 'Let the worst hap, thou canst but meet thy fate.'

CREON What is thy news? Why this despondency?

GUARD Let me premise a word about myself? I neither did the deed nor saw it done, Nor were it just that I should come to harm.

CREON Thou art good at parry, and canst fence about Some matter of grave import, as is plain.

GUARD The bearer of dread tidings needs must quake.

CREON Then, sirrah, shoot thy bolt and get thee gone.

GUARD Well, it must out; the corpse is buried; someone E'en now besprinkled it with thirsty dust, Performed the proper ritual--and was gone.

CREON What say'st thou? Who hath dared to do this thing?

GUARD I cannot tell, for there was ne'er a trace Of pick or mattock--hard unbroken ground, Without a scratch or rut of chariot wheels, No sign that human hands had been at work. When the first sentry of the morning watch Gave the alarm, we all were terror-stricken. The corpse had vanished, not interred in earth, But strewn with dust, as if by one who sought To avert the curse that haunts the unburied dead: Of hound or ravening jackal, not a sign. Thereat arose an angry war of words; Guard railed at guard and blows were like to end it, For none was there to part us, each in turn Suspected, but the guilt brought home to none, From lack of evidence. We challenged each The ordeal, or to handle red-hot iron, Or pass through fire, affirming on our oath Our innocence--we neither did the deed Ourselves, nor know who did or compassed it. Our quest was at a standstill, when one spake And bowed us all to earth like quivering reeds, For there was no gainsaying him nor way To escape perdition: Yeareboundtotell TheKing,yecannothideit; so he spake. And he convinced us all; so lots were cast, And I, unlucky scapegoat, drew the prize. So here I am unwilling and withal Unwelcome; no man cares to hear ill news.

CHORUS I had misgivings from the first, my liege, Of something more than natural at work.

CREON O cease, you vex me with your babblement; I am like to think you dote in your old age. Is it not arrant folly to pretend That gods would have a thought for this dead man? Did they forsooth award him special grace, And as some benefactor bury him, Who came to fire their hallowed sanctuaries, To sack their shrines, to desolate their land, And scout their ordinances? Or perchance The gods bestow their favors on the bad. No! no! I have long noted malcontents Who wagged their heads, and kicked against the yoke, Misliking these my orders, and my rule. 'Tis they, I warrant, who suborned my guards By bribes. Of evils current upon earth The worst is money. Money 'tis that sacks Cities, and drives men forth from hearth and home; Warps and seduces native innocence, And breeds a habit of dishonesty. But they who sold themselves shall find their greed Out-shot the mark, and rue it soon or late. Yea, as I still revere the dread of Zeus, By Zeus I swear, except ye find and bring Before my presence here the very man Who carried out this lawless burial, Death for your punishment shall not suffice. Hanged on a cross, alive ye first shall make Confession of this outrage. This will teach you What practices are like to serve your turn. There are some villainies that bring no gain. For by dishonesty the few may thrive, The many come to ruin and disgrace.

GUARD May I not speak, or must I turn and go Without a word?--

CREON   Begone! canst thou not see That e'en this question irks me?

GUARD   Where, my lord? Is it thy ears that suffer, or thy heart?

CREON Why seek to probe and find the seat of pain?

GUARD I gall thine ears--this miscreant thy mind.

CREON What an inveterate babbler! get thee gone!

GUARD Babbler perchance, but innocent of the crime.

CREON Twice guilty, having sold thy soul for gain.

GUARD Alas! how sad when reasoners reason wrong.

CREON Go, quibble with thy reason. If thou fail'st To find these malefactors, thou shalt own The wages of ill-gotten gains is death. [Exit CREON]

GUARD I pray he may be found. But caught or not (And fortune must determine that) thou never Shalt see me here returning; that is sure. For past all hope or thought I have escaped, And for my safety owe the gods much thanks.

CHORUS (Str. 1) Many wonders there be, but naught more wondrous than man; Over the surging sea, with a whitening south wind wan, Through the foam of the firth, man makes his perilous way; And the eldest of deities Earth that knows not toil nor decay Ever he furrows and scores, as his team, year in year out, With breed of the yoked horse, the ploughshare turneth about.

(Ant. 1) The light-witted birds of the air, the beasts of the weald and the wood He traps with his woven snare, and the brood of the briny flood. Master of cunning he: the savage bull, and the hart Who roams the mountain free, are tamed by his infinite art; And the shaggy rough-maned steed is broken to bear the bit.

(Str. 2) Speech and the wind-swift speed of counsel and civic wit, He hath learnt for himself all these; and the arrowy rain to fly And the nipping airs that freeze, 'neath the open winter sky. He hath provision for all: fell plague he hath learnt to endure; Safe whate'er may befall: yet for death he hath found no cure.

(Ant. 2) Passing the wildest flight thought are the cunning and skill, That guide man now to the light, but now to counsels of ill. If

he honors the laws of the land, and reveres the Gods of the State
Proudly his city shall stand; but a cityless outcast I rate Whoso
bold in his pride from the path of right doth depart; Ne'er may I sit
by his side, or share the thoughts of his heart.

What strange vision meets my eyes, Fills me with a wild sur-
prise? Sure I know her, sure 'tis she, The maid Antigone.
Hapless child of hapless sire, Didst thou recklessly conspire,
Madly brave the King's decree? Therefore are they haling thee?
[Enter GUARD bringing ANTIGONE]

GUARD Here is the culprit taken in the act Of giving burial.
But where's the King?

CHORUS There from the palace he returns in time. [Enter
CREON]

CREON Why is my presence timely? What has chanced?

GUARD No man, my lord, should make a vow, for if He ever
swears he will not do a thing, His afterthoughts belie his first resolve. When from the hail-storm of thy threats I fled I sware thou
wouldst not see me here again; But the wild rapture of a glad surprise Intoxicates, and so I'm here forsworn. And here's my prisoner, caught in the very act, Decking the grave. No lottery this time;
This prize is mine by right of treasure-trove. So take her, judge her,
rack her, if thou wilt. She's thine, my liege; but I may rightly claim
Hence to depart well quit of all these ills.

CREON Say, how didst thou arrest the maid, and where?

GUARD Burying the man. There's nothing more to tell.

CREON Hast thou thy wits?   Or know'st thou what thou
say'st?

GUARD I saw this woman burying the corpse Against thy orders. Is that clear and plain?

CREON But how was she surprised and caught in the act?

GUARD It happened thus. No sooner had we come, Driven
from thy presence by those awful threats, Than straight we swept
away all trace of dust, And bared the clammy body. Then we sat
High on the ridge to windward of the stench, While each man kept
he fellow alert and rated Roundly the sluggard if he chanced to
nap. So all night long we watched, until the sun Stood high in

heaven, and his blazing beams Smote us. A sudden whirlwind then uppraised A cloud of dust that blotted out the sky, And swept the plain, and stripped the woodlands bare, And shook the firmament. We closed our eyes And waited till the heaven-sent plague should pass. At last it ceased, and lo! there stood this maid. A piercing cry she uttered, sad and shrill, As when the mother bird beholds her nest Robbed of its nestlings; even so the maid Wailed as she saw the body stripped and bare, And cursed the ruffians who had done this deed. Anon she gathered handfuls of dry dust, Then, holding high a well-wrought brazen urn, Thrice on the dead she poured a lustral stream. We at the sight swooped down on her and seized Our quarry. Undismayed she stood, and when We taxed her with the former crime and this, She disowned nothing. I was glad--and grieved; For 'tis most sweet to 'scape oneself scot-free, And yet to bring disaster to a friend Is grievous. Take it all in all, I deem A man's first duty is to serve himself.

CREON Speak, girl, with head bent low and downcast eyes, Does thou plead guilty or deny the deed?

ANTIGONE Guilty. I did it, I deny it not.

CREON (to GUARD) Sirrah, begone whither thou wilt, and thank Thy luck that thou hast 'scaped a heavy charge. (To AN-TIGONE) Now answer this plain question, yes or no, Wast thou acquainted with the interdict?

ANTIGONE I knew, all knew; how should I fail to know?

CREON And yet wert bold enough to break the law?

ANTIGONE Yea, for these laws were not ordained of Zeus, And she who sits enthroned with gods below, Justice, enacted not these human laws. Nor did I deem that thou, a mortal man, Could'st by a breath annul and override The immutable unwritten laws of Heaven. They were not born today nor yesterday; They die not; and none knoweth whence they sprang. I was not like, who feared no mortal's frown, To disobey these laws and so provoke The wrath of Heaven. I knew that I must die, E'en hadst thou not proclaimed it; and if death Is thereby hastened, I shall count it gain. For death is gain to him whose life, like mine, Is full of misery. Thus my lot appears Not sad, but blissful; for had I endured To leave my mother's son unburied there, I should have grieved with reason, but not now. And if in this thou judgest me a fool, Methinks the judge of folly's not acquit.

CHORUS A stubborn daughter of a stubborn sire, This ill-starred maiden kicks against the pricks.

CREON Well, let her know the stubbornest of wills Are soonest bended, as the hardest iron, O'er-heated in the fire to brittleness, Flies soonest into fragments, shivered through. A snaffle curbs the fieriest steed, and he Who in subjection lives must needs be meek. But this proud girl, in insolence well-schooled, First overstepped the established law, and then-- A second and worse act of insolence-- She boasts and glories in her wickedness. Now if she thus can flout authority Unpunished, I am woman, she the man. But though she be my sister's child or nearer Of kin than all who worship at my hearth, Nor she nor yet her sister shall escape The utmost penalty, for both I hold, As arch-conspirators, of equal guilt. Bring forth the older; even now I saw her Within the palace, frenzied and distraught. The workings of the mind discover oft Dark deeds in darkness schemed, before the act. More hateful still the miscreant who seeks When caught, to make a virtue of a crime.

ANTIGONE Would'st thou do more than slay thy prisoner?

CREON Not I, thy life is mine, and that's enough.

ANTIGONE Why dally then? To me no word of thine Is pleasant: God forbid it e'er should please; Nor am I more acceptable to thee. And yet how otherwise had I achieved A name so glorious as by burying A brother? so my townsmen all would say, Where they not gagged by terror, Manifold A king's prerogatives, and not the least That all his acts and all his words are law.

CREON Of all these Thebans none so deems but thou.

ANTIGONE These think as I, but bate their breath to thee.

CREON Hast thou no shame to differ from all these?

ANTIGONE To reverence kith and kin can bring no shame.

CREON Was his dead foeman not thy kinsman too?

ANTIGONE One mother bare them and the self-same sire.

CREON Why cast a slur on one by honoring one?

ANTIGONE The dead man will not bear thee out in this.

CREON Surely, if good and evil fare alive.

ANTIGONE The slain man was no villain but a brother.

CREON The patriot perished by the outlaw's brand.

ANTIGONE Nathless the realms below these rites require.

CREON Not that the base should fare as do the brave.

ANTIGONE Who knows if this world's crimes are virtues there?

CREON Not even death can make a foe a friend.

ANTIGONE My nature is for mutual love, not hate.

CREON Die then, and love the dead if thou must; No woman shall be the master while I live. [Enter ISMENE]

CHORUS Lo from out the palace gate, Weeping o'er her sister's fate, Comes Ismene; see her brow, Once serene, beclouded now, See her beauteous face o'erspread With a flush of angry red.

CREON Woman, who like a viper unperceived Didst harbor in my house and drain my blood, Two plagues I nurtured blindly, so it proved, To sap my throne. Say, didst thou too abet This crime, or dost abjure all privity?

ISMENE I did the deed, if she will have it so, And with my sister claim to share the guilt.

ANTIGONE That were unjust. Thou would'st not act with me At first, and I refused thy partnership.

ISMENE But now thy bark is stranded, I am bold To claim my share as partner in the loss.

ANTIGONE Who did the deed the under-world knows well: A friend in word is never friend of mine.

ISMENE O sister, scorn me not, let me but share Thy work of piety, and with thee die.

ANTIGONE Claim not a work in which thou hadst no hand; One death sufficeth. Wherefore should'st thou die?

ISMENE What would life profit me bereft of thee?

ANTIGONE Ask Creon, he's thy kinsman and best friend.

ISMENE Why taunt me? Find'st thou pleasure in these

gibes?

ANTIGONE 'Tis a sad mockery, if indeed I mock.

ISMENE O say if I can help thee even now.

ANTIGONE No, save thyself; I grudge not thy escape.

ISMENE Is e'en this boon denied, to share thy lot?

ANTIGONE Yea, for thou chosed'st life, and I to die.

ISMENE Thou canst not say that I did not protest.

ANTIGONE Well, some approved thy wisdom, others mine.

ISMENE But now we stand convicted, both alike.

ANTIGONE Fear not; thou livest, I died long ago Then when I gave my life to save the dead.

CREON Both maids, methinks, are crazed. One suddenly Has lost her wits, the other was born mad.

ISMENE Yea, so it falls, sire, when misfortune comes, The wisest even lose their mother wit.

CREON I' faith thy wit forsook thee when thou mad'st Thy choice with evil-doers to do ill.

ISMENE What life for me without my sister here?

CREON Say not thy sister here: thy sister's dead.

ISMENE What, wilt thou slay thy own son's plighted bride?

CREON Aye, let him raise him seed from other fields.

ISMENE No new espousal can be like the old.

CREON A plague on trulls who court and woo our sons.

ANTIGONE O Haemon, how thy sire dishonors thee!

CREON A plague on thee and thy accursed bride!

CHORUS What, wilt thou rob thine own son of his bride?

CREON 'Tis death that bars this marriage, not his sire.

CHORUS So her death-warrant, it would seem, is sealed.

CREON By you, as first by me; off with them, guards, And keep them close. Henceforward let them learn To live as women use, not roam at large. For e'en the bravest spirits run away When they perceive death pressing on life's heels.

CHORUS (Str. 1) Thrice blest are they who never tasted pain! If once the curse of Heaven attaint a race, The infection lingers on and speeds apace, Age after age, and each the cup must drain.

So when Etesian blasts from Thrace downpour Sweep o'er the blackening main and whirl to land From Ocean's cavernous depths his ooze and sand, Billow on billow thunders on the shore.

(Ant. 1) On the Labdacidae I see descending Woe upon woe; from days of old some god Laid on the race a malison, and his rod Scourges each age with sorrows never ending.

The light that dawned upon its last born son Is vanished, and the bloody axe of Fate Has felled the goodly tree that blossomed late. O Oedipus, by reckless pride undone!

(Str. 2) Thy might, O Zeus, what mortal power can quell? Not sleep that lays all else beneath its spell, Nor moons that never tire: untouched by Time, Throned in the dazzling light That crowns Olympus' height, Thou reignest King, omnipotent, sublime.

Past, present, and to be, All bow to thy decree, All that exceeds the mean by Fate Is punished, Love or Hate.

(Ant. 2) Hope flits about never-wearying wings; Profit to some, to some light loves she brings, But no man knoweth how her gifts may turn, Till 'neath his feet the treacherous ashes burn. Sure 'twas a sage inspired that spake this word; If evil good appear To any, Fate is near; And brief the respite from her flaming sword.

Hither comes in angry mood Haemon, latest of thy brood; Is it for his bride he's grieved, Or her marriage-bed deceived, Doth he make his mourn for thee, Maid forlorn, Antigone? [Enter HAEMON]

CREON Soon shall we know, better than seer can tell. Learning may fixed decree anent thy bride, Thou mean'st not, son, to rave against thy sire? Know'st not whate'er we do is done in love?

HAEMON O father, I am thine, and I will take Thy wisdom as the helm to steer withal. Therefore no wedlock shall by me be held More precious than thy loving goverance.

CREON Well spoken: so right-minded sons should feel, In all deferring to a father's will. For 'tis the hope of parents they may rear A brood of sons submissive, keen to avenge Their father's wrongs, and count his friends their own. But who begets unprofitable sons, He verily breeds trouble for himself, And for his foes much laughter. Son, be warned And let no woman fool away thy wits. Ill fares the husband mated with a shrew, And her embraces very soon wax cold. For what can wound so surely to the quick As a false friend? So spue and cast her off, Bid her go find a husband with the dead. For since I caught her openly rebelling, Of all my subjects the one malcontent, I will not prove a traitor to the State. She surely dies. Go, let her, if she will, Appeal to Zeus the God of Kindred, for If thus I nurse rebellion in my house, Shall not I foster mutiny without? For whoso rules his household worthily, Will prove in civic matters no less wise. But he who overbears the laws, or thinks To overrule his rulers, such as one I never will allow. Whome'er the State Appoints must be obeyed in everything, But small and great, just and unjust alike. I warrant such a one in either case Would shine, as King or subject; such a man Would in the storm of battle stand his ground, A comrade leal and true; but Anarchy-- What evils are not wrought by Anarchy! She ruins States, and overthrows the home, She dissipates and routs the embattled host; While discipline preserves the ordered ranks. Therefore we must maintain authority And yield to title to a woman's will. Better, if needs be, men should cast us out Than hear it said, a woman proved his match.

CHORUS To me, unless old age have dulled wits, Thy words appear both reasonable and wise.

HAEMON Father, the gods implant in mortal men Reason, the choicest gift bestowed by heaven. 'Tis not for me to say thou errest, nor Would I arraign thy wisdom, if I could; And yet wise thoughts may come to other men And, as thy son, it falls to me to mark The acts, the words, the comments of the crowd. The commons stand in terror of thy frown, And dare not utter aught that might offend, But I can overhear their muttered plaints, Know how the people mourn this maiden doomed For noblest deeds to die the worst of deaths. When her own brother slain in battle lay Unsepulchered, she suffered not his corse To lie for carrion birds and dogs to maul: Should not her name (they cry) be writ in gold? Such the low murmurings that reach my ear. O father, nothing is by me more prized Than thy well-being, for what higher good Can children covet than their sire's fair fame, As fathers too take pride in glorious sons?

Therefore, my father, cling not to one mood, And deemed not thou art right, all others wrong. For whoso thinks that wisdom dwells with him, That he alone can speak or think aright, Such oracles are empty breath when tried. The wisest man will let himself be swayed By others' wisdom and relax in time. See how the trees beside a stream in flood Save, if they yield to force, each spray unharmed, But by resisting perish root and branch. The mariner who keeps his mainsheet taut, And will not slacken in the gale, is like To sail with thwarts reversed, keel uppermost. Relent then and repent thee of thy wrath; For, if one young in years may claim some sense, I'll say 'tis best of all to be endowed With absolute wisdom; but, if that's denied, (And nature takes not readily that ply) Next wise is he who lists to sage advice.

CHORUS If he says aught in season, heed him, King. (To HAEMON) Heed thou thy sire too; both have spoken well.

CREON What, would you have us at our age be schooled, Lessoned in prudence by a beardless boy?

HAEMON I plead for justice, father, nothing more. Weigh me upon my merit, not my years.

CREON Strange merit this to sanction lawlessness!

HAEMON For evil-doers I would urge no plea.

CREON Is not this maid an arrant law-breaker?

HAEMON The Theban commons with one voice say, No.

CREON What, shall the mob dictate my policy?

HAEMON 'Tis thou, methinks, who speakest like a boy.

CREON Am I to rule for others, or myself?

HAEMON A State for one man is no State at all.

CREON The State is his who rules it, so 'tis held.

HAEMON As monarch of a desert thou wouldst shine.

CREON This boy, methinks, maintains the woman's cause.

HAEMON If thou be'st woman, yes. My thought's for thee.

CREON O reprobate, would'st wrangle with thy sire?

HAEMON Because I see thee wrongfully perverse.

CREON And am I wrong, if I maintain my rights?

HAEMON Talk not of rights; thou spurn'st the due of Heaven

CREON O heart corrupt, a woman's minion thou!

HAEMON Slave to dishonor thou wilt never find me.

CREON Thy speech at least was all a plea for her.

HAEMON And thee and me, and for the gods below.

CREON Living the maid shall never be thy bride.

HAEMON So she shall die, but one will die with her.

CREON Hast come to such a pass as threaten me?

HAEMON What threat is this, vain counsels to reprove?

CREON Vain fool to instruct thy betters; thou shall rue it.

HAEMON Wert not my father, I had said thou err'st.

CREON Play not the spaniel, thou a woman's slave.

HAEMON When thou dost speak, must no man make reply?

CREON This passes bounds. By heaven, thou shalt not rate And jeer and flout me with impunity. Off with the hateful thing that she may die At once, beside her bridegroom, in his sight.

HAEMON Think not that in my sight the maid shall die, Or by my side; never shalt thou again Behold my face hereafter. Go, consort With friends who like a madman for their mate. [Exit HAEMON]

CHORUS Thy son has gone, my liege, in angry haste. Fell is the wrath of youth beneath a smart.

CREON Let him go vent his fury like a fiend: These sisters twain he shall not save from death.

CHORUS Surely, thou meanest not to slay them both?

CREON I stand corrected; only her who touched The body.

CHORUS And what death is she to die?

CREON She shall be taken to some desert place By man untrod, and in a rock-hewn cave, With food no more than to avoid the taint That homicide might bring on all the State, Buried alive. There let her call in aid The King of Death, the one god she reveres, Or learn too late a lesson learnt at last: 'Tis labor lost, to reverence the dead.

CHORUS (Str.) Love resistless in fight, all yield at a glance of thine eye, Love who pillowed all night on a maiden's cheek dost lie, Over the upland holds. Shall mortals not yield to thee?

(Ant). Mad are thy subjects all, and even the wisest heart Straight to folly will fall, at a touch of thy poisoned dart. Thou didst kindle the strife, this feud of kinsman with kin, By the eyes of a winsome wife, and the yearning her heart to win. For as her consort still, enthroned with Justice above, Thou bendest man to thy will, O all invincible Love.

Lo I myself am borne aside, From Justice, as I view this bride. (O sight an eye in tears to drown) Antigone, so young, so fair, Thus hurried down Death's bower with the dead to share.

ANTIGONE (Str. 1) Friends, countrymen, my last farewell I make; My journey's done. One last fond, lingering, longing look I take At the bright sun. For Death who puts to sleep both young and old Hales my young life, And beckons me to Acheron's dark fold, An unwed wife. No youths have sung the marriage song for me, My bridal bed No maids have strewn with flowers from the lea, 'Tis Death I wed.

CHORUS But bethink thee, thou art sped, Great and glorious, to the dead. Thou the sword's edge hast not tasted, No disease thy frame hath wasted. Freely thou alone shalt go Living to the dead below.

ANTIGONE (Ant. 1) Nay, but the piteous tale I've heard men tell Of Tantalus' doomed child, Chained upon Siphylus' high rocky fell, That clung like ivy wild, Drenched by the pelting rain and whirling snow, Left there to pine, While on her frozen breast the tears aye flow-- Her fate is mine.

CHORUS She was sprung of gods, divine, Mortals we of mortal line.Like renown with gods to gain Recompenses all thy pain. Take this solace to thy tomb Hers in life and death thy doom.

ANTIGONE (Str. 2) Alack, alack! Ye mock me. Is it meet

Thus to insult me living, to my face? Cease, by our country's altars I entreat, Ye lordly rulers of a lordly race. O fount of Dirce, wood-embowered plain Where Theban chariots to victory speed, Mark ye the cruel laws that now have wrought my bane, The friends who show no pity in my need! Was ever fate like mine? O monstrous doom, Within a rock-built prison sepulchered, To fade and wither in a living tomb, And alien midst the living and the dead.

CHORUS (Str. 3) In thy boldness over-rash Madly thou thy foot didst dash 'Gainst high Justice' altar stair. Thou a father's guild dost bear.

ANTIGONE (Ant. 2) At this thou touchest my most poignant pain, My ill-starred father's piteous disgrace, The taint of blood, the hereditary stain, That clings to all of Labdacus' famed race. Woe worth the monstrous marriage-bed where lay A mother with the son her womb had borne, Therein I was conceived, woe worth the day, Fruit of incestuous sheets, a maid forlorn, And now I pass, accursed and unwed, To meet them as an alien there below; And thee, O brother, in marriage ill-bestead, 'Twas thy dead hand that dealt me this death-blow.

CHORUS Religion has her chains, 'tis true, Let rite be paid when rites are due. Yet is it ill to disobey The powers who hold by might the sway. Thou hast withstood authority, A self-willed rebel, thou must die.

ANTIGONE Unwept, unwed, unfriended, hence I go, No longer may I see the day's bright eye; Not one friend left to share my bitter woe, And o'er my ashes heave one passing sigh.

CREON If wail and lamentation aught availed To stave off death, I trow they'd never end. Away with her, and having walled her up In a rock-vaulted tomb, as I ordained, Leave her alone at liberty to die, Or, if she choose, to live in solitude, The tomb her dwelling. We in either case Are guiltless as concerns this maiden's blood, Only on earth no lodging shall she find.

ANTIGONE O grave, O bridal bower, O prison house Hewn from the rock, my everlasting home, Whither I go to join the mighty host Of kinsfolk, Persephassa's guests long dead, The last of all, of all more miserable, I pass, my destined span of years cut short. And yet good hope is mine that I shall find A welcome from my sire, a welcome too, From thee, my mother, and my brother dear; From with these hands, I laved and decked your limbs In death, and poured libations on your grave. And last, my Polyneices, unto thee I paid due rites, and this my recompense! Yet am I justified in wisdom's eyes. For even had it been some child of mine, Or husband mouldering in death's decay, I had not wrought this deed despite the State. What is the law I call in aid? 'Tis thus I argue. Had it been a husband dead I might have wed another, and have borne Another child, to take the dead child's place. But, now my sire and mother both are dead, No second brother can be born for me. Thus by the law of conscience I was led To honor thee, dear brother, and was judged By Creon guilty of a heinous crime. And now he drags me like a criminal, A bride unwed, amerced of marriage-song And marriage-bed and joys of motherhood, By friends deserted to a living grave. What ordinance of heaven have I transgressed? Hereafter can I look to any god For succor, call on any man for help? Alas, my piety is impious deemed. Well, if such justice is approved of heaven, I shall be taught by suffering my sin; But if the sin is theirs, O may they suffer No worse ills than the wrongs they do to me.

CHORUS The same ungovernable will Drives like a gale the maiden still.

CREON Therefore, my guards who let her stay Shall smart full sore for their delay.

ANTIGONE Ah, woe is me! This word I hear Brings death most near.

CHORUS I have no comfort. What he saith, Portends no other thing than death.

ANTIGONE My fatherland, city of Thebes divine, Ye gods of Thebes whence sprang my line, Look, puissant lords of Thebes, on me; The last of all your royal house ye see. Martyred by men of sin, undone. Such meed my piety hath won. [Exit ANTIGONE]

CHORUS (Str. 1) Like to thee that maiden bright, Danae, in her brass-bound tower, Once exchanged the glad sunlight For a cell, her bridal bower. And yet she sprang of royal line, My child, like thine, And nursed the seed By her conceived Of Zeus descending in a golden shower. Strange are the ways of Fate, her power Nor wealth, nor arms withstand, nor tower; Nor brass-prowed ships, that breast the sea From Fate can flee.

(Ant. 1) Thus Dryas' child, the rash Edonian King, For words of high disdain Did Bacchus to a rocky dungeon bring, To cool the madness of a fevered brain. His frenzy passed, He learnt at last 'Twas madness gibes against a god to fling. For once he fain had quenched the Maenad's fire; And of the tuneful Nine provoked the ire.

(Str. 2) By the Iron Rocks that guard the double main, On Bosporus' lone strand, Where stretcheth Salmydessus' plain I n the wild Thracian land, There on his borders Ares witnessed The vengeance by a jealous step-dame ta'en The gore that trickled from a spindle red, The sightless orbits of her step-sons twain.

(Ant. 2) Wasting away they mourned their piteous doom, The blasted issue of their mother's womb. But she her lineage could trace To great Erecththeus' race; Daughter of Boreas in her sire's vast caves Reared, where the tempest raves, Swift as his horses o'er the hills she sped; A child of gods; yet she, my child, like thee, By Destiny That knows not death nor age--she too was vanquished. [Enter TEIRESIAS and BOY]

TEIRESIAS Princes of Thebes, two wayfarers as one, Having betwixt us eyes for one, we are here. The blind man cannot move without a guide.

CREON Why tidings, old Teiresias?

TEIRESIAS I will tell thee; And when thou hearest thou must heed the seer.

CREON Thus far I ne'er have disobeyed thy rede.

TEIRESIAS So hast thou steered the ship of State aright.

CREON I know it, and I gladly own my debt.

TEIRESIAS Bethink thee that thou treadest once again The razor edge of peril.

CREON What is this? Thy words inspire a dread presentiment.

TEIRESIAS The divination of my arts shall tell. Sitting upon my throne of augury, As is my wont, where every fowl of heaven Find harborage, upon mine ears was borne A jargon strange of twitterings, hoots, and screams; So knew I that each bird at the other tare With bloody talons, for the whirr of wings Could signify naught else. Perturbed in soul, I straight essayed the sacrifice by fire On blazing altars, but the God of Fire Came not in flame, and from the thigh bones dripped And sputtered in the ashes a foul ooze; Gall-bladders cracked and spurted up: the fat Melted and fell and left the thigh bones bare. Such are the signs, taught by this lad, I read-- As I guide others, so the boy guides me-- The frustrate signs of oracles grown dumb. O King, thy willful temper ails the State, For all our shrines and altars are profaned By what has filled the maw of dogs and crows, The flesh of Oedipus' unburied son. Therefore the angry gods abominate Our litanies and our burnt offerings; Therefore no birds trill out a happy note, Gorged with the carnival of human gore. O ponder this, my son. To err is common To all men, but the man who having erred Hugs not his errors, but repents and seeks The cure, is not a wastrel nor unwise. No fool, the saw goes, like the obstinate fool. Let death disarm thy vengeance. O forbear To vex the dead. What glory wilt thou win By slaying twice the slain? I mean thee well; Counsel's most welcome if I promise gain.

CREON Old man, ye all let fly at me your shafts Like anchors at a target; yea, ye set Your soothsayer on me. Peddlers are ye all And I the merchandise ye buy and sell. Go to, and make your profit where ye will, Silver of Sardis change for gold of Ind; Ye will not purchase this man's burial, Not though the winged ministers of Zeus Should bear him in their talons to his throne; Not e'en in awe of prodigy so dire Would I permit his burial, for I know No human soilure can assail the gods; This too I know, Teiresias, dire's the fall Of craft and cunning when it tries to gloss Foul treachery with fair words for filthy gain.

TEIRESIAS Alas! doth any know and lay to heart--

CREON Is this the prelude to some hackneyed saw?

TEIRESIAS How far good counsel is the best of goods?

CREON True, as unwisdom is the worst of ills.

TEIRESIAS Thou art infected with that ill thyself.

CREON I will not bandy insults with thee, seer.

TEIRESIAS And yet thou say'st my prophesies are frauds.

CREON Prophets are all a money-getting tribe.

TEIRESIAS And kings are all a lucre-loving race.

CREON Dost know at whom thou glancest, me thy lord?

TEIRESIAS Lord of the State and savior, thanks to me.

CREON Skilled prophet art thou, but to wrong inclined.

TEIRESIAS Take heed, thou wilt provoke me to reveal The mystery deep hidden in my breast.

CREON Say on, but see it be not said for gain.

TEIRESIAS Such thou, methinks, till now hast judged my words.

CREON Be sure thou wilt not traffic on my wits.

TEIRESIAS Know then for sure, the coursers of the sun Not many times shall run their race, before Thou shalt have given the fruit of thine own loins In quittance of thy murder, life for life; For that thou hast entombed a living soul, And sent below a denizen of earth, And wronged the nether gods by leaving here A corpse unlaved, unwept, unsepulchered. Herein thou hast no part, nor e'en the gods In heaven; and thou usurp'st a power not thine. For this the avenging spirits of Heaven and Hell Who dog the steps of sin are on thy trail: What these have suffered thou shalt suffer too. And now, consider whether bought by gold I prophesy. For, yet a little while, And sound of lamentation shall be heard, Of men and women through thy desolate halls; And all thy neighbor States are leagues to avenge Their mangled warriors who have found a grave I' the maw of wolf or hound, or winged bird That flying homewards taints their city's air. These are the shafts, that like a bowman I Provoked to anger, loosen at thy breast, Unerring, and their smart thou shalt not shun. Boy, lead me home, that he may vent his spleen On younger men, and learn to curb his tongue With gentler manners than his present mood. [Exit TEIRESIAS]

CHORUS My liege, that man hath gone, foretelling woe. And, O believe me, since these grizzled locks Were like the raven, never have I known The prophet's warning to the State to fail.

CREON I know it too, and it perplexes me. To yield is grievous, but the obstinate soul That fights with Fate, is smitten grievously.

CHORUS Son of Menoeceus, list to good advice.

CHORUS What should I do. Advise me. I will heed.

CHORUS Go, free the maiden from her rocky cell; And for the

unburied outlaw build a tomb.

CREON Is that your counsel? You would have me yield?

CHORUS Yea, king, this instant. Vengeance of the gods Is
swift to overtake the impenitent.

CREON Ah! what a wrench it is to sacrifice My heart's resolve;
but Fate is ill to fight.

CHORUS Go, trust not others. Do it quick thyself.

CREON I go hot-foot. Bestir ye one and all, My henchmen!
Get ye axes! Speed away To yonder eminence! I too will go, For all
my resolution this way sways. 'Twas I that bound, I too will set her
free. Almost I am persuaded it is best To keep through life the law
ordained of old. [Exit CREON]

CHORUS (Str. 1) Thou by many names adored, Child of Zeus
the God of thunder, Of a Theban bride the wonder, Fair Italia's
guardian lord;

In the deep-embosomed glades Of the Eleusinian Queen Haunt
of revelers, men and maids, Dionysus, thou art seen.

Where Ismenus rolls his waters, Where the Dragon's teeth
were sown, Where the Bacchanals thy daughters Round thee
roam,   There thy home; Thebes, O Bacchus, is thine own.

(Ant. 1) Thee on the two-crested rock Lurid-flaming torches see;
Where Corisian maidens flock, Thee the springs of Castaly.

By Nysa's bastion ivy-clad, By shores with clustered vineyards
glad, There to thee the hymn rings out, And through our streets we
Thebans shout, All hall to thee Evoe, Evoe!

(Str. 2) Oh, as thou lov'st this city best of all, To thee, and to
thy Mother levin-stricken, In our dire need we call; Thou see'st
with what a plague our townsfolk sicken. Thy ready help we crave,
Whether adown Parnassian heights descending, Or o'er the roar-
ing straits thy swift was wending, Save us, O save!

(Ant. 2) Brightest of all the orbs that breathe forth light,   Au-
thentic son of Zeus, immortal king, Leader of all the voices of the
night, Come, and thy train of Thyiads with thee bring, Thy   maddened rout Who dance before thee all night long, and shout,
Thy handmaids we, Evoe, Evoe!

[Enter MESSENGER]

MESSENGER Attend all ye who dwell beside the halls Of Cadmus and Amphion. No man's life As of one tenor would I praise or blame, For Fortune with a constant ebb and rise Casts down and raises high and low alike, And none can read a mortal's horoscope. Take Creon; he, methought, if any man, Was enviable. He had saved this land Of Cadmus from our enemies and attained A monarch's powers and ruled the state supreme, While a right noble issue crowned his bliss. Now all is gone and wasted, for a life Without life's joys I count a living death. You'll tell me he has ample store of wealth, The pomp and circumstance of kings; but if These give no pleasure, all the rest I count The shadow of a shade, nor would I weigh His wealth and power 'gainst a dram of joy.

CHORUS What fresh woes bring'st thou to the royal house?

MESSENGER Both dead, and they who live deserve to die.

CHORUS Who is the slayer, who the victim? speak.

MESSENGER Haemon; his blood shed by no stranger hand.

CHORUS What mean ye? by his father's or his own?

MESSENGER His own; in anger for his father's crime.

CHORUS O prophet, what thou spakest comes to pass.

MESSENGER So stands the case; now 'tis for you to act.

CHORUS Lo! from the palace gates I see approaching Creon's unhappy wife, Eurydice. Comes she by chance or learning her son's fate? [Enter EURYDICE]

EURYDICE Ye men of Thebes, I overheard your talk. As I passed out to offer up my prayer To Pallas, and was drawing back the bar To open wide the door, upon my ears There broke a wail that told of household woe Stricken with terror in my handmaids' arms I fell and fainted. But repeat your tale To one not unacquaint with misery.

MESSENGER Dear mistress, I was there and will relate The perfect truth, omitting not one word. Why should we gloze and flatter, to be proved Liars hereafter? Truth is ever best. Well, in attendance on my liege, your lord, I crossed the plain to its utmost margin, where The corse of Polyneices, gnawn and mauled, Was lying yet. We offered first a prayer To Pluto and the goddess of cross-ways, With contrite hearts, to deprecate their ire. Then laved with lustral waves the mangled corse, Laid it on fresh-lopped branches, lit a pyre, And to his memory piled a mighty mound Of mother earth. Then to the caverned rock, The bridal chamber of the maid and Death, We sped, about to enter. But a guard Heard from that godless shrine a far shrill wail, And ran back to our lord to tell the news. But as he nearer drew a hollow sound Of lamentation to the King was borne. He groaned and uttered then this bitter plaint: "Am I a prophet? miserable me! Is this the saddest path I ever trod? 'Tis my son's voice that calls me. On press on, My henchmen, haste with double speed to the tomb Where rocks down-torn have made a gap, look in And tell me if in truth I recognize The voice of Haemon or am heaven-deceived." So at the bidding of our distraught lord We looked, and in the craven's vaulted gloom I saw the maiden lying strangled there, A noose of linen twined about her neck; And hard beside her, clasping her cold form, Her lover lay bewailing his dead bride Death-wedded, and his father's cruelty. When the King saw him, with a terrible groan He moved towards him, crying, "O my son What hast thou done? What ailed thee? What mischance Has reft thee of thy reason? O come forth, Come forth, my son; thy father supplicates." But the son glared at him with tiger eyes, Spat in his face, and then, without a word, Drew his two-hilted sword and smote, but missed His father flying backwards. Then the boy, Wroth with himself, poor wretch, incontinent Fell on his sword and drove it through his side Home, but yet breathing clasped in his lax arms The maid, her pallid cheek incarnadined With his expiring gasps. So there they lay Two corpses, one in death. His marriage rites Are consummated in the halls of Death: A witness that of ills whate'er befall Mortals' unwisdom is the worst of all. [Exit EURY-DICE]

CHORUS What makest thou of this? The Queen has gone Without a word importing good or ill.

MESSENGER I marvel too, but entertain good hope. 'Tis that she shrinks in public to lament Her son's sad ending, and in privacy Would with her maidens mourn a private loss. Trust me, she is discreet and will not err.

CHORUS I know not, but strained silence, so I deem, Is no less ominous than excessive grief.

MESSENGER Well, let us to the house and solve our doubts, Whether the tumult of her heart conceals Some fell design. It may be thou art right: Unnatural silence signifies no good.

CHORUS Lo! the King himself appears. Evidence he with him bears 'Gainst himself (ah me! I quake 'Gainst a king such charge to make) But all must own, The guilt is his and his alone.

CREON (Str. 1) Woe for sin of minds perverse, Deadly fraught with mortal curse. Behold us slain and slayers, all akin. Woe for my counsel dire, conceived in sin. Alas, my son, Life scarce begun, Thou wast undone. The fault was mine, mine only, O my son!

CHORUS Too late thou seemest to perceive the truth.

CREON (Str. 2) By sorrow schooled. Heavy the hand of God, Thorny and rough the paths my feet have trod, Humbled my pride, my pleasure turned to pain; Poor mortals, how we labor all in vain! [Enter SECOND MESSENGER]

SECOND MESSENGER Sorrows are thine, my lord, and more to come, One lying at thy feet, another yet More grievous waits thee, when thou comest home.

CREON What woe is lacking to my tale of woes?

SECOND MESSENGER Thy wife, the mother of thy dead son here, Lies stricken by a fresh inflicted blow.

CREON (Ant. 1) How bottomless the pit! Does claim me too, O Death? What is this word he saith, This woeful messenger? Say, is it fit To slay anew a man already slain? Is Death at work again, Stroke upon stroke, first son, then mother slain?

CHORUS Look for thyself. She lies for all to view.

CREON (Ant. 2) Alas! another added woe I see. What more remains to crown my agony? A minute past I clasped a lifeless son, And now another victim Death hath won. Unhappy mother, most unhappy son!

SECOND MESSENGER Beside the altar on a keen-edged sword She fell and closed her eyes in night, but erst She mourned for Megareus who nobly died Long since, then for her son; with her last breath She cursed thee, the slayer of her child.

CREON (Str. 3) I shudder with affright O for a two-edged sword to slay outright A wretch like me, Made one with misery.

SECOND MESSENGER 'Tis true that thou wert charged by

the dead Queen As author of both deaths, hers and her son's.

CREON In what wise was her self-destruction wrought?

SECOND MESSENGER Hearing the loud lament above her son With her own hand she stabbed herself to the heart.

CREON (Str. 4) I am the guilty cause. I did the deed, Thy murderer. Yea, I guilty plead. My henchmen, lead me hence, away, away, A cipher, less than nothing; no delay!

CHORUS Well said, if in disaster aught is well His past endure demand the speediest cure.

CREON (Ant. 3)   Come, Fate, a friend at need,   Come with all speed!   Come, my best friend, And speed my end! Away, away! Let me not look upon another day!

CHORUS This for the morrow; to us are present needs That they whom it concerns must take in hand.

CREON I join your prayer that echoes my desire.

CHORUS O pray not, prayers are idle; from the doom Of fate for mortals refuge is there none.

CREON (Ant. 4) Away with me, a worthless wretch who slew Unwitting thee, my son, thy mother too. Whither to turn I know now; every way Leads but astray, And on my head I feel the heavy weight Of crushing Fate.

CHORUS Of happiness the chiefest part Is a wise heart: And to defraud the gods in aught With peril's fraught. Swelling words of high-flown might Mightily the gods do smite. Chastisement for errors past Wisdom brings to age at last.

Made in United States
North Haven, CT
17 February 2023